STRANGER THINGIES

JOHN BIRMINGHAM is a journalist, columnist, blogger, prolific tweeter and author of two Quarterly Essays, a number of books of fiction, non-fiction and memoir. These include *He Died with a Felafel in His Hand*, *The Tasmanian Babes Fiasco*, the Axis of Time series of thrillers, the Disappearance series and the Dave Hooper novels. He won the National Award for Non-Fiction with *Leviathan: The Unauthorised Biography of Sydney*. *How To Be a Writer: Who Smashes Deadlines, Crushes Editors and Lives in a Solid Gold Hovercraft* was published in 2016. He currently writes regular columns for Fairfax Media.

JOHN BIRMINGHAM

STRANGER THINGIES

FROM *FELAFEL* TO NOW

NEWSOUTH

A NewSouth book

Published by
NewSouth Publishing
University of New South Wales Press Ltd
University of New South Wales
Sydney NSW 2052
AUSTRALIA
newsouthpublishing.com

National Library of Australia
Cataloguing-in-Publication entry
Creator: Birmingham, John, 1964- author.
Title: Stranger Thingies / John Birmingham.
ISBN: 9781742235592 (paperback)
        9781742244013 (ebook)
        9781742248394 (epdf)
Subjects: Birmingham, John, 1964-
Australian literature--Collections.
Authors--Australia--Miscellanea.
Authors, Australian.

Design Josephine Pajor-Markus
Cover design Luke Causby, Blue Cork
Printer Griffin Press

UNSW
SYDNEY

CONTENTS

Introduction

Stephen King once made the point that horror and humour are two of the most difficult writing forms. Done poorly, horror turns unintentionally funny. And bad humour is just creepy.

As I write these words decades after I first put pen to paper – actual ink to actual paper – I find myself recalling that when I started writing, I wanted to be Stephen King. To write horror stories.

So yeah. That didn't work out too well.

You can see my first attempt in the State Library of New South Wales. I donated a handwritten manuscript of terrible quality, based on second-hand ideas stolen directly from the early works of the King. It's inspirational. Reading it, a young author could not help but think, 'Sweet baby cheeses, this loser is even worse than I *thought*. If he can get published, I'll probably be able to buy JK Rowling's Scottish castle with my royalties.'

And maybe you will. Best of luck to you, kid.

I gave up on horror writing, although I did circle

back around a ways with the Dave Hooper series. Those books, about a massive douchebag accidentally embiggened into a superhero, have all the trappings of horror novels: vampires, zombies, deplorable rednecks with no sense of irony. But they're played for lulz. These, it turns out, are easier than scares. At least for me.

It's telling, I think, that I grubbed around as a starving freelancer for ten years before Michael Duffy published *He Died with a Felafel in His Hand*. I was a very successful freelancer, which meant I was making about twelve grand a year and eating a lot of two-dollar meals at the Hare Krishna cafe in Kings Cross. The sultana pudding was nice, fuck you very much.

But after *Felafel*, I never ate there again. Not even for the pudding. I could afford to buy real pudding at grown-up restaurants where they won't even let you in the front door if you're not wearing big-boy pants and shoes.

What changed?

It wasn't just the enormous royalty cheques Michael signed every six months.

It was the lulz.

After *Felafel*, editors paid me for the lulz, not for the stories. Because as the King pointed out, horror and humour are damned hard work. Not once a day, in a tweet or something. Anybody can do that. But when you have to crank thousands of words a week, every week, or you end up living under a bridge and dreaming of the days when you could afford two-dollar cult pudding for lunch, then being funny is hard and sometimes hateful work.

You can spend hours working on a single joke and I will put money on the barrelhead that within an hour or so of it being released into the world some buzz-killing shithead will front you to tell you it wasn't funny. (Trust me, kid. It was funny. The buzzkiller's got deeper issues he's working through.) Sometimes you'll toss off some half-baked idea leading up to the real pay-off and it's the asinine, undeveloped joke that gets all the ROFLs.

Don't sweat that, either. Making people laugh, or smile, or just quietly taking them out of whatever shitty day they're having, that's good honest work. You probably won't be remembered for it, but that doesn't matter. When you check out you'll have done more good in the world than harm. Be content with that.

The pieces collected here span over 20 years of writing. They make their way in from the fringe press, where I started out writing for food vouchers, and they include some of the most recent work I've done in a private column, written only for paying subscribers.

That's how this business has gone. Originally, if you had a knack for making people smile and occasionally laugh you could aspire to a weekly column somewhere, the closest thing to regular work a grinning bullshitter can hope for outside of telemarketing or politics. That sort of gig is getting to be rare, though. I have one with Fairfax, at *Brisbane Times*, which I've been doing for ten years and still enjoy. But one by one, the magazines and newspapers which used to be the natural home of the pro satirist have died or gone digital. They can only pay in 'exposure'.

Still, I'm cranking out many more jokes per week than I ever have, and the repo men haven't come for me yet. Long after I'm gone I feel pretty confident plenty of others will be making the rent in the same racket.

The thing which has really changed isn't the business model of the mainstream media (Google ate that years ago). It's the connection to your readers, to the people you're trying to amuse. It used to be that the only way you knew a joke had landed − like, really knew − was when you were lucky enough to see somebody reading your stuff in public and laughing.

That's some powerful juju, right there − faintly, distantly akin to the magic a stand-up comedian taps into when they're in front of a full house and riding the laughs like a surf break at Mavericks. I don't know how stand-ups do it, but I can understand why it would be so addictive, and so utterly destructive too.

They're mainlining a drug that writers of humour, alone at their keyboards and disconnected from immediate feedback, can taste only in severely diluted form, at least until recently. Somebody once told me that a small piece I'd written called 'Consider the bucket bong' for a now defunct mag was the funniest thing they'd ever read, but they told me months after it came out. That piece became the inspiration for *Felafel*, and as well as that book did, it was still months before I had any direct experience of its success.

These days, people come at you within seconds to let you know what they thought. My particular heroin is to hear, usually on Twitter, that somebody snorted coffee through their nose when reading my morning column.

It sounds a little needy, when I look at it on the page. But I can cop to that. There is an egomaniacal hunger to all writing, but especially to this sort. It is possible to write poetry and literature for yourself. Honestly, people do it all the time. But I don't think anybody ever wrote a joke, a sketch or a line of satire for purely private pleasure. To be fully appreciated, humour must be shared. It is one of those rare things from which you gain the most by giving it up to the world.

So, I'm giving you these pieces, collected over many years. I hope you'll find most of them funny. I know one or two will slip past you, because in the end the necessarily shared subjectivity of humour rules out a comprehensive universality. That's a mighty wanky way of saying 'to each their own', especially with jokes.

If there is but one thing I'd like to take away from all this, besides the massive royalty payments, it's the satisfaction of knowing that I brightened an otherwise shitty day for somebody somewhere.

THE THINGS THEMSELVES

If magazines profiled men like women

Guy Manfellow is waiting for me at the bar of a stylishly obscure bar. It is quiet, perhaps only half the seats are taken, but every head in the stylishly obscure bar is turned just a little way towards Manfellow, every eye drawn to his long legs, carefully crossed at well-turned ankles. It's the legs you notice first.

Guy Manfellow's legs are long and his ankles, if you could see them beneath the black dress socks poking out from beneath the cuffs of his perfectly pressed Ralph Lauren pants ... well, those ankles are perfect.

Guy Manfellow smiles when I mention his perfect ankles.

'Everyone says that,' he smiles, and his smile is kind, if a little weary at fending off compliments all day. 'But I'm about more than my ankles.'

Yes, yes he is. Guy Manfellow is a very important man who does things – important things involving other things. But none of those things are as important right now as the powerful thighs I see stretching the fabric of his pants like old redwoods wrapped in

Indian cotton, or perhaps his calves, which are famously so geometrically perfect that evolutionary scientists and intelligent designers both cite them in arguments in favour of their position.

We meet because Manfellow's important thing that he is being important about is more important during the next two weeks than at most other times of the year, when he remains important but without something to sell.

It's winter, but there is no chill anywhere in this bar because Manfellow is steaming it up. His very presence raises the ambient temperature, but in one of those meta-fame moments that must frame every day in the life of a man as important as Manfellow, his image appears on the wide flat screen of one of the televisions suspended over the bar.

There is Manfellow, hovering over Manfellow, steaming up the pages of *Man Monthly Magazine*'s February issue with a super-sexy photo shoot that features the important and powerful man we know as Manfellow in little more than his underpants.

Somebody starts clapping and a woman across the bar wolf-whistles.

'You'd be surprised how often that happens,' says Manfellow.

No, no I would not, because I am sitting across from Guy Manfellow and I cannot keep my eyes off him. My eyes are drawn up the inverted V-shape of his flat stomach and wide flaring shoulders; they hurry past the genuinely shocking symmetry of his face. The same small, wry curve bends his lips up on the left as it does on the right. He has two eyes and they are the same colour. His brow, which furrows when he thinks about all the things for which he is important, is perfectly balanced, like a problem of logic that can only be solved by the furrowing of Guy Manfellow's brow in this exact fashion.

He is handsome, of course. But you knew that. You knew it because the truth of it leached into you from a thousand magazine covers, and a million online photos and hundreds of YouTube videos. What you didn't know is that Guy Manfellow's particular type of handsome is closer to the sublime, to a force of nature, like a tsunami of handsome sweeping down his face and across the subject—object division that separates you from him and him from the imperfect world in which he must exist as the sole example of handsome perfection.

'Are we going to talk about my thing?' he asks, all business. Say one thing about Guy Manfellow, and if it isn't something about his ankles or thighs or rock-hard abs, it's that Guy Manfellow is all business. In an industry of high-stakes deals about things, Manfellow wears his carefully tailored image as a man who does important things as carefully as the carefully tailored shirt that barely hides the barely hidden power of his powerful upper body. His full head of hair is both soft and hard, because he is a man of contrasts.

His partners, and there have been many, have been women of contrasts: millionaire ladies and celebrity florists. He never talks about them, but it doesn't matter because we do and will in a separate breakout article for each of the best looking women to have been associated with Manfellow, or even rumoured to have been associated with him. Even if we made up the rumour ourselves.

They're important, these women, because when it comes to important men doing things, we cannot help but be preoccupied with their image, their age, their weight, whether they have had children or not, and whether they regret not having children.

Manfellow doesn't buy into it. He's the age he is and he's looking good. The women he dates are also looking good. So good they make him look even better, as if this were possible. His face shows no sign of cosmetic surgery; rather, he simply looks like someone who takes good care of himself. He walks with a self-confidence that says 'I take good care of myself'. And as if to make that point, last year, he wore a black tuxedo to the Thing Awards and he looked good. Very good.

'I'm no male model', he says. 'I have wrinkles. But being a man who does things, it hasn't been an issue and I've not been made to feel like I need to go to the nearest plastic surgeon. Who cares at this point? This is me.'

Yes, yes it is. This is Guy Manfellow. He does things.

Sun-Herald, February 2014

Batten down the hashtags

The storm of controversy began early. Much earlier than the moment at which the first gust of wind tugged at the trending topics; well before a few drops of forboding rain spotted a single Facebook timeline. What started it? Well, somebody said something wrong on the internet, we know that much for sure. Or maybe somebody did something wrong and somebody else said something about it on the internet? And it was #notcool and they wouldn't even apologise. Or something. What mattered was ... it had begun.

The storm of controversy.

Or rather #TheControversy.

(And also #TheThing, which was a little bit smaller and less important to everyone except those poor souls who came late and didn't realise #TheControversy was the thing that was happening today, and having committed to #TheThing they could hardly then move to #TheControversy because all of their best snark, and the retweet they got from the celebrity who liked their snarky comment about #TheThing, would be lost.)

From this small, almost infinitesimal nothing, a great maelstrom grew. A vast, angry world-spanning storm, drawing in millions, then hundreds of millions as it roared and raged. A storm of controversy so vast and destructive that it would generate memes – yes, actual memes! – before its savagery was spent. And those memes would tear across the world, sucking up thousands of retweets and likes like a giant storm-pocalypse, even before Mr Bolt at Mr Murdoch's electronical newsheets hunkered down under the lashing fury and mounting snark to courageously hoist up a blogpost condemning #theirABC for the whole thing.

Oh. My. God. Omigod omigod omigod.

So sexist.

So racist.

So homophobic.

Oh no! He did not!?! gasped the internet, eyes squeezed shut, head turned away from the horror of the page views.

Oh yes he did, howled the internet, and it was all undeniably Mia Freedman's fault. The storm of controversy was reaching peak fury now, gross outrage sheeting in horizontally as Tumblrs launched that very day crashed against WordPress blogs creaking with age and festooned with mouldering banner ads, but captained by old salts who'd seen it all before. They knew what to do. They turned right for the towering

black wave of increased traffic. Their meme genera-
tors redlined to pump out the lulz. Their hardiest trolls
slaved down in the engine room, stoking the fires of
controversy with oily barrels of incendiary bile.

But their efforts were as nothing compared to the
juggernaut of BuzzFeed, which not only caught the
rising storm of controversy and whipped it up with
secret algorithms and '24 Insanely Simple Ways to
Whip Up a Storm of Controversy', but surfed the dangerous surge right past the Venerable Old Masthead,
which was so firmly anchored to the bedrock of its traditional heritage that its poor befuddled master editor
didn't even know #TheControversy was happening.
Already leaking readers and losing younger members
of the crew overboard, many of them paddling franti-
cally after the receding BuzzFeed, the Venerable Old
Masthead gamely persisted with its important coverage of a local council plan to introduce paid parking
to a street which didn't always have paid parking.

Those poor brave bastards never knew what swept
away their readers.

It was the storm of controversy. Now grown to
such ferocity that GetUp! launched a petition and
Helen Razer was forced to rage-quit Twitter again
so that she might find a quiet and safe harbour in
which to write a very, very long op-ed piece about how
the ferocity of #TheControversy was fundamentally

misdirected because it missed the underlying economic fractures which actually divide all from all. Feminists were appalled. Activists were appalled. GetUp! launched another petition and Razer was forced to defend triple j's playlist while the storm of controversy raged around them all.

Of course, this could only make things worse. Horribly, horribly worse, and at this critical point in the storm of controversy the only thing that could have made things even more worserer (which is an actual internet word, so shut up, you) was Mia Freedman tweeting something.

At that very moment, at the shrieking height of the storm of controversy, Mia Freedman tweeted something.

Oh noes! And now, even though it was just a retweet and a Facebook link to Mamamia's article '24 Insanely Stupid Things We Did to Whip Up a Storm of Controversy', it was every man for himself, which opened a new storm front in #TheControversy because of the gratuitously sexist and offensive implications of not letting every woman be for herself. The Men's Rights Movement suddenly hove into view, and pulled their fighting socks all the way up from their sandals to decry the blatant misandry of everything.

The storm of controversy now calved little stormlets, fractal tempests within the greater tempest. A gay man from Africa made the very important point that as a gay man from Africa he thought the plight of gay men from Africa had been completely written out of the narrative of #TheControversy. The most important blogger in the Fat Acceptance Movement wrote a post proving that the fat-hate of the thin-privileged, which had been lurking just below the surface of #TheControversy, was an even more important controversy than the original controversy. Tony Abbott refused to say anything about the controversy, which only showed yet again that he was the worst prime minister in Australian history. Kochie caused a laff-riot on *Sunrise* by tricking Sammy into doing another pole-dancing thing because, 'Er, controversy', grinned Kochie.

Finally, nearly 12 hours after the storm of controversy broke, the drenching spittle ceased to fly, the hot air cooled down, and #TheControversy slowly slipped below the horizon of trending topics and popular posts. Because something else was on the telly.

But none who lived through it would ever forget the storm of controversy, until a day or two later, three at the most, when somebody said something wrong on the internet, or they did something and it was #notcool and they wouldn't even apologise. Or something. What mattered was ... it had begun again.

Sun-Herald, January 2014

Precious freedom thingies

Like you, I often find myself wandering the streets of our fair city wondering, what can I do to protect our precious Aussie way of life? 'Fuckin' heaps!' is the answer, especially if I'm carrying a can of spray paint and there's a handy mosque nearby. Nothing threatens our precious Aussie freedoms and ways as much as a nearby mosque that hasn't been spray-painted with slogans like 'Get the fuck out of our country'. Unless of course it's a mosque which has threatened our precious ways and thingies by not being spray-painted with the warning that 'Muslims are evil and have no respect for our ways'.

Crikey, that sort of thing just burns me up. We didn't fight Hitler at Gallipoli just so a bunch of Muslims could come here to disrespect our ways and thingies.

It's a short rough ride down a long slippery slope from letting Muslims say prayers and stuff, in sheds that haven't been vandalised, to Muslim ladies openly walking the streets like they're allowed to or something.

It's like they think they can come to this free country,
or even be born here, and walk around without decent
Aussies being allowed to yell at them. They seem to
forget that if they were in Saudi Arabia they wouldn't
even have the freedom to stop at a traffic light on Been-
leigh Road and have hot coffee thrown at them by a
real, freedom-loving Aussie. The sort of Aussie who
cherishes the freedom to mistake one sort of brown
person for another on the Gold Coast and threaten to
cut his head off because he looked like a Muslim …
and they cut people's heads off.

I hear these stories and it stirs my heart, as it surely
does yours. How could you not love a country that
loves the freedom thingy so much?

And when I think of the threat to our precious
thingies from a dangerous Muslim lady walking openly
around West End in a headscarf, I thank God – the
real God, not that made-up one in the jihad beard –
that the spirit of Myall Creek still burns in a few sun-
tanned hearts and some brave son of Anzac had the
courage to confront her and tell her he wanted to burn
her murderous headscarf.

It's only by constant vigilance and standing up
for our most cherished thingies that we can stop these
intolerant Muslims from subverting all the thingies
Breaker Morant fought so hard to protect in Viet-
nam. Our ways and thingies and precious, precious

freedoms. The freedom to spit at brown people in the street. The freedom to just make shit up about them and call it news. To spray rude words on their places of worship.

Australians all let us rejoice.

brisbanetimes.com.au, September 2014

Why I miss the '90s

It is time. Every decade gets its comeback and it is time for the '90s Revival. We should do it for the kids.

For those of you who weren't there, my little Millennial friends, sit back in this complimentary Hypercolor T-shirt and enjoy a leftover Vanilla Coke while I wrestle a couple of episodes of *Buffy* I taped into my video-playing apparatus. This technology plays actual tapes, and that's why we say we'll 'tape' *BoJack Horseman* rather than, 'I will digitally store a perfect copy of the ones and zeroes which, properly formatted, will play back a *BoJack Horseman* episode from my drive, stick or legitimate streaming service.'

You see Buffy there, kids? She's the reason you have female heroes worth watching these days, when you are actually lucky enough to have them, of course. Buffy's what you get in a just world, where sparkly vampires aren't even a thing and Marvel Comics hasn't decided that all female action heroes are lycra-clad sex dolls.

Now, don't listen to those awful Gen Y types, kids.

They're still recovering from the shock of finding out that corner offices, annual bonuses and promiscuous job hopping aren't naturally occurring economic phenomena.

Listen to your Uncle JB instead while I tell you about a very special time that we should all miss, even though you weren't there. This was *Buffy* time. And Keating time, and the three-buck-fifty ham and cheese croissant. Who was this Keating?

Oh man, he was this awesome mash-up of Tywin Lannister, the new Doctor Who's sweariest YouTube videos and Agent Smith from *The Matrix*. (Just Google that last one.) He made the '90s something to miss now.

There were other great things that happened all the time in the '90s. You could drink all night and not wake up with a hangover. You didn't need to exercise because *Aerobics Oz Style* took care of that on the TV. You could get a coffee for two bucks, or even a buck eighty, to go with that cheap ham and cheese croissant. And if you got tired of cheap ham and cheese croissants – I know, like that would ever happen, right? – you could switch up to a focaccia, which was a type of bread so versatile you could toast it as a sandwich, or sleep on it as a surprisingly comfortable if high-carb mattress.

In the '90s, kids, we had a thing called optimism, which you guys would really love. The Gen Ys sort of mistook optimism for a reason to demand all the corner offices on their first day at work, but I don't imagine you Millennials would do that. Not after 17 years of war and terror and the celebrated theft of trillions of dollars' worth of pure wealth by one-tenth of 1 per cent of the world's rich bastards. Optimism was what we had before they cut people's heads off on the internet. And before we bombed everyone everywhere so they wouldn't do that sort of thing any more.

Yeah, you'd love '90s optimism, kids. It sounded like disco, which is another thing from history, but not from the '90s.

Optimism was big things, like not even worrying about getting your head cut off on the internet, or somebody deciding to blow up half a country where that happened. And it was little things, like knowing a new episode of *Seinfeld* was coming and that it would be awesome. Did you know the word awesome was invented in the '90s, kids? We had to invent it because it described the state of knowing that Mulder and Scully would totally do it one day, even if there was a sudden time dilation and nobody could even remember it happening.

Optimism was going to Barons up the Cross or the Story Bridge Bomb Shelter and thinking it would turn out right, and of course it would, because Ben Folds Five was on the radio and it was like a party in the cab on the way there. Optimism was your mood ring and your sneakers which lit up. It was unironic scrunchies at war with The Rachel haircut. And Discman players that would never, ever eat your mixtape.

You would have loved the '90s, kids. It was a special time. And I miss it very much.

brisbanetimes.com.au, August 2014

Hip hop is old-people music now

This is horrifying. Not Mick Fanning shark punch-up horrifying. This is worse. Hip hop is now old-people music. I would run into the sea and punch all the sharks to make this go away, but I cannot. Not because I'm afraid of sharks but because HIP HOP IS NOW OLD-PEOPLE MUSIC.

How do we know this? Because the *New York Times* told us, and the *New York Times* is the journal of record for everything old-people related.

This weekend just past the *Times'* old-people music correspondent, Alex French, reported at length on the sudden and unexpected emergence of radio stations playing nothing but 'classic hip-hop'. These stations were not gnarly little underground start-ups netcasting the most rabid and revolutionary tracks from the violent front of America's class and race wars.

Nope. They were previously failing mainstream outlets, often run by a robot's playlist of endless loops of adult contemporary snoozak. Now they play acceptable hip hop. Because acceptable hip hop is the new solid-gold classics for old people.

It all started with WRWM, Indianapolis's 15th-most-popular radio station, which is to say it started somewhere akin to Adelaide's lowest rated contemporary Christian rock cover-band station.

And it has since taken over the airwaves, everywhere. What happened there will happen here.

Because hip hop is now all about the golden oldies.

WRWM's parent company, a giant conglomerate which owns more than 450 stations, tried an experiment with its central Indiana stinker – a radio station so bereft of ideas that it once broadcast TV show themes for weeks on end, before trying out the market for nonstop construction noises. The experiment was a holiday weekend of 'classic hip-hop'.

Long story short, they buried the competition and they're still doing it.

From the *Times*:

The DJ dropped the needle on Naughty by Nature's 'Hip Hop Hooray' at 3 p.m. on Dec. 19. LL Cool J's 'Around the Way Girl' followed, then 'Move,' by Ludacris. 'We set up a voicemail box for listener feedback,' Michaels said. 'I was expecting lots of complaints. We went from playing Maroon 5 to "Me So Horny".' The phone rang so much they had to clear the mailbox every day. Callers were ecstatic.

The station never returned to its old format. In three weeks, 93.9 made the improbable jump from 15th place in Central Indiana to first.

Why? Because hip hop is cool? I want to say yes, but the answer is no. Because apparently hip hop is now for old people, who were cool when they were listening to hip hop in the 1990s.

Two. Decades. Ago.

But now hip hop is the background hum of harried parents and overstressed mortgage holders as they rush from school pick-up to the kids' soccer practice to the supermarket for a jumbo box of fish fingers – friend of delinquent parents everywhere.

As old-people musical correspondent Alex French explains, since the dawn of Rock, time has eventually worn all the sharp edges off the hardest edged music. 'Thirty years ago, young listeners of hip-hop, with its predilection for violent imagery and unprintable language, might have thought it impervious to this process. But radio conglomerates are proving them wrong … It now qualifies as oldies.'

Oh Snoop Dogg, how could you do this to me?

I was ready for the sun to go down on Nirvana. I could face the long dark night of Blink-182's inevitable eclipse. But you, Dawg. And you, Hoodies. I thought you could keep me cool forever.

If you'll excuse me I'm going to play some Eagles albums. The live sets. With the clunky wooden onstage banter. Apparently it's all I have left.

brisbanetimes.com.au, July 2015

How Big Waterbed sprung a leak

It is no coincidence that the decline of *Playboy* mag-azine, the Playboy Mansion, and the associated hydra-headed conglomerate of *Playboy*-related limited liability companies tracks almost exactly the collapse of the waterbed market. Once a multibillion-dollar colossus, Big Waterbed is now a soggy, deflated bladder leaking regret and shame over the mouldy shag-pile carpet of our defeated culture.

Once upon a time, the late 1980s in fact, water-beds were the Pokémon Go of bedtime technology.

Now waterbeds are the Pokémon Go of bedtime technology.

The insanity has passed and millions who once proudly insisted on the wettest bed possible are like, 'Wait! What? No, that wasn't me.'

What happened, waterbed people? How did it all go so horribly wrong?

Well, *Playboy* didn't help, which is to say Hugh Hefner didn't help. The modern, temperature-controlled waterbed was invented by Charles Hall, a

Californian grad student, in 1968. Hall built one for his master's thesis in design. He was and remains seriously committed to the potential of the waterbed as an elegant reimagining of a banal but universal domestic furnishing.

By 1970, Maximum Playboy Hugh Hefner boasted two aircraft carrier–sized waterbeds at the Playboy Mansion, one covered in livid green velvet and the other in luxurious possum fur imported from far Tasmania. It meant doom for Hall's utilitarian vision of the waterbed. With Hef and his Bunnies enthusiastically surfing this new wave, what self-respecting 1970s orgy guy or miniskirted sex mama would not want to get down on that all-you-can-eat booty buffet?

Sadly, this sort of thing happens all the time. Dr John Kellogg famously developed his celebrated cornflake as a sex antidote, to discourage the early morning masturbatory impulse through the power of the cornflakes' crispy crushing dullness. Then his greedy brother William added a metric shit-tonne of irresistible sugar to every packet and millions of American perverts were soon mouth-hoovering the sweet-'n'-sexy pornflakes out of each other's Brazilian crevices and pubic forests.

That's exactly what happened to waterbeds too.

For 20 years waterbeds were the Bunk Town express. In 1986, the *New York Times* even considered them a significant enough item of design – like an Eames Chair or the original iPod – to be worthy of historically interrogating the form. They seemed to capture the spirit of the age, wrote the *Times*, 'filled with up to 250 gallons of water and who knows how many tons of sexual promise'.

Donkaliciousness duly authenticated by America's paper of record, the waterbed died screaming in the windowless dungeon of the *Times*' legendary clueless-ness shortly after.

The time of the waterbed people had already passed. They were heavy, they leaked everywhere, and they were actually really, really bad for sex. The beds weren't much good either, other than as visual punchlines for lazy sitcom writers who were forever introducing them to cats with extra-sharp claws. From a glorious peak, where every fourth or fifth bed in the free world was a hypnotically undulating latex orgy bladder, the waterbed passed into history.

My mother-in-law still has one, and two cats, and a puncture repair kit.

The action at bedtime has moved on, but not too far. The hippest development in the land of nod right now? Sand bed mattresses, which are not a million miles removed from Charles Hall's grad project. Conceptually, they're just up the beach from it. And, just like the waterbed, what chance the sand mattress will be sold as a therapeutic aid for the treatment of pressure sores and tricky backs when it could be more profitably advertised as an enormously heavy and inconvenient sexual platform on which to relive teen-age dreams of getting some at the beach?

aliensideboob.com, January 2017

Hotel beds are the best beds

Are you sitting down? Science has proven sex is better in hotel beds. Well, okay, one scientist. Alright then, a sex therapist. On the internet. But he has actual sciencey reasons. Hotels are not simply a novel setting, far removed from the unwashed doona, covered in cat hair and old chocolate wrappers, where you do it in your socks once or twice a month, when you can be bothered taking off your shoes. Hotel rooms are fantastically luxurious settings, and when they're not, even better – the thrill of a bit of rough is still a thrill.

But I don't think this valuable research has gone quite far enough. Sure, sex in a hotel bed might turn jungle mad and dangerously animated after a long spell of phoning it in, but it's not just sex. Everything is better in a hotel bed. PJ O'Rourke once observed that the fastest cars in the world are rental cars. I propose as a corollary that the bounciest beds are hotel beds. Memory foam trampolines, they are. Springy enough with a good run-up to propel you right across the room into the pillow fort you've constructed from every available pillow on the hotel's pillow menu. (Pro tip: you get what you pay for with pillow menus. Five- and six-star prices should guarantee a vast degustation menu of pillowy goodness. A twenty-buck stay in a fugitive motel will probably mean building your fort out of wadded-up toilet paper. It won't be soft toilet paper either.)

In a good hotel bed you can eat whole cartons of extra-crumbly chocolate chip biscuits because a good hotel bed will be so ridiculously fucking large that entire biscuit cantonments can be set aside to host the crumbs. Do you know how many pizzas you can eat in a hotel bed? Wrong question. You should first ask yourself what is the limit on your credit card and, then, what is that limit divided by the price of a pizza delivered right to my hotel bed by room service. Comfort-food binges in hotel beds are better than comfort-food binges in your bed because there is no theoretical limit to the binge, only the practical limit of how much you can pay for, unless you are on expenses, in which case your hotel bed becomes PJ O'Rourke's rental car of lying around eating things.

Likewise, Netflix binges in hotel beds are better than Netflix binges at home because there's no chance of being interrupted by crying children with incon- venient night terrors. Fancy a little *Game of Thrones* cosplay in your hotel bed? Room service will be right up with another gourd of Cersei's favourite Dornish Strongwine – 'as dark as blood and as sweet as vengeance'. (See also earlier ref to hotel bed rumpy pumpy.)

From providing a large and pliable playing surface on which to re-create the Battle of Austerlitz, with hotel mini-bar bottles taking the role of the various French, Russian and Austrian army units, to simply sleeping in because you can, nothing beats a hotel bed. Your hotel bed will not lie there, reproachfully unmade, if you lie there, disgracefully undressed atop it until lunchtime. At some point the hotel bed fairies will arrive and make it up for you again.

It is as close to heaven as you will ever get on this earth.

smh.com.au, November 2015

Fox in socks and sandals

When it comes to crimes against fashion I confess to being a serial offender. Most days I can't even dress like a grown-up. In winter I rarely get out of my cheeky monkey PJs and bathrobe. Come summer there'd better be a damn good reason to wear anything but board shorts and old T-shirts with faded beer adverts on them. But even I do not wear socks with sandals. Even I know not to do that.

Not ever.

Not while wrapped in a Snuggie. Not while pondering the chances of getting a third week out of the same unwashed tracky dacks. (The chances, since you ask, are very good.) Not even while deranged with bath salts and eating the face of random passers-by. There are some things, like wearing socks with sandals, that you simply don't do.

But this season, according to no lesser style fascists than Calvin Klein, Bottega Veneta, *Out Magazine* and the febrile hive mind of New York Fashion Week, this is exactly what we are supposed to do. The *Wall*

Street Journal, indeed, reports that this year models are slinking their way down the catwalk in haute couture and socks and sandals. It was allegedly a stylistic development first seen among American footballers who, being large and violent, were not stopped when they should have been.

The *Journal* reported the so-called thoughts of a Mr Brandon Meriweather, eight-year veteran of the NFL, who said 'athletes say they wear socks with sandals because they can ... It's nice to relax their toes.'

Well yes, I'm sure it is, and given the high incidence of acquired brain injuries among professional footballers, it's even explicable. But that doesn't make it right.

What is next?

Perhaps cardigans? Don't think I didn't notice when secret commissions from Big Cardy forced even James Bond into one of the sad-looking things in *Quantum of Solace.* Certainly, it was a very natty cardigan, but a cardigan it remained, and once having donned the favoured leisure wear of balding accountants everywhere, it cannot be long before you succumb to socks and sandals, 007. Indeed, why stop there? Why not sandals and leg warmers? Perhaps teamed with a pastel-coloured suit jacket, the sleeves of which have been rolled up 1980s style.

Remembers the 1980s? The time that taste forgot?

Even in the 1980s people knew better than to wear socks with sandals.

Perhaps having crossed this Rubicon we will rush towards something really spectacular. Like knotted handkerchiefs on the bonce and long trousers rolled up above the knee, all the better to show off one's expensive, bespoke leather sandals and colourfully crazy socks, perhaps held up with a fetching black garter? Yes, that is almost certainly next, because 'fashion consultant' Nick Wooster was still included in *Vanity Fair*'s 2015 International Best-Dressed List after 'wearing toeless green socks with orange stripes along with gray, double-strapped sandals'.

You know it's going to happen, even if the horror is a little muted as Target dilutes the trend for the mass market. This time next year you will be stepping out looking like a sunburned German tourist with no idea. And I will be judging you. In my tracky dacks.

The Age, October 2015

Johnny Depp robbed my car

I woke up yesterday morning to discover my car had been broken into and Johnny Depp was in town. I make no allegations and draw no conclusions about this. I do note, however, that my car has sat unmolested in the driveway for over a year, never once having drawn the attention of ruffians or ne'er-do-wells. I further note that Mr Depp, who sometimes prefers to go by the alias Cap'n Jack Sparrow, is well known as a pirate, and furthermore it is well known that pirates are exactly the sorts of reprobates one might expect to find rustling through the cup holder of one's automobile with a view to trousering the loose change.

The fact that the loose change was not actually taken is very suspicious. Mr Depp is a wealthy man and would not need the $1.37 in small coins I had left in the cup holder to cover any emergencies.

Indeed, not much was taken from my car, even though it was very obviously broken into, with the doors left ajar, the glove box opened and emptied, and my unrivalled collection of old chocolate bar wrappers and non-deductible tax receipts missing. I deduce that the thieves – and I stress I make no allegations or insinuations of any kind as to their identity – that the thieves simply crammed everything into one discarded plastic shopping bag to effect their escape and inspect their loot later.

I know there was more than one thief because both the driver- and passenger-side doors were open. I also note, for no particular reason, that Mr Depp did not arrive alone in this country. He travelled in league with his longtime accomplice Ms Heard.

Two prominent bad eggs.

Two car doors ajar this morning.

No! No, I do not mean to imply anything about this remarkable concurrence of events or the 100 per cent correlation between instances of Mr Depp and Ms Heard arriving in the local area yesterday and my car being broken into at the same time.

I have spoken to the police about the mysterious fact that nothing other than a lot of old rubbish was taken, but they seemed remarkably uninterested in the crime or some very obvious leads they might have followed that would have led them to the Southport Magistrates Court.

For example, I had one CD in the back of the glove box. A collection of independently produced hip hop tracks from emerging Logan MCs. It was not stolen. And here is a fascinating coincidence: extensive Google searches have failed to reveal even one occasion when Mr Depp expressed any interest in taking or even borrowing a collection of independently produced Aussie hip hop tracks from emerging Logan MCs. For that matter, Ms Heard, who is better known in Queensland legal circles as 'the accused', has likewise never once mentioned an interest in Logan's independent hip hop scene.

A competent detective might make something of this unusual correlation of facts, but I will not hold my breath. It seems Queensland's finest are all busy taking selfies with the accused and her collaborator.

It is not all gloom and thievery in my world, though. I still have my collection of independently produced hip hop tracks from emerging Logan MCs. It's out the front, in the car. The doors are unlocked. There is no alarm system.

brisbanetimes.com.au, April 2016

An extraordinary meeting of the Bounders Club

Re: Finances

I draw your attention to the only matter on tonight's agenda, the treacherous treachery of those Blackguards and Villains in the Athenaeum Club who have split off to form their own association (moments before they could be run off at bayonet point, I do not need to add but will) over the issue of female ladies being allowed as members.

Please, gentlemen, please! Could we possibly hold it down to a decorous roar of disapproval, if you please? I hope I do not need to remind any of you of the rule against discharging large-bore shotguns in the library. Again.

Thank you.

Now, if I might. I have here, I am afraid to say, a parchment from our colleagues in the Athenaeum, and the Melbourne Club, with a sticky note from Tatt's attached, seeking our support in reproving and demurring from any approach by these ne'er-do-wells of this so-called Melbourne Forum, who will of course be looking for allies in their preposterous shenanigans.

Good sirs, I find myself horrified, and horribly so, that such communications should even be thought of as necessary where the good offices and intentions of the Bounders are concerned. By Grabthar's Hammer I demand to know why on earth they would have even felt it warranted the effort to ask.

My fellow Bounders, do we have a traitor amongst us? Is there even one of you here tonight who has toyed with the profanity of even thinking about the merest possibility of admitting the lady folk to these our hallowed halls? Well? Let's hear it.

You, Lord Bob of Nowhere? It's no secret you entertain some dangerously liberal ideas. Have you entered into some form of obscene intercourse with these upstart fellows and their censorious, hairy-legged, she-wolf puppeteers?

Would you have us all drowning in the library or trophy room under torrents of potpourri and inane nattering that simply circles around and around the same blasted topic like a riding elephant with an enormous eye patch never getting to the bloody point as though the damned circling and yapping and yapping and circling about the blasted thing *was* the very point of it? Well? Would you? Because that is what will become of us if we are to throw our lot in with these effete Lady Men of this so-called new club.

Gadzooks, we shall not have it, sirs. The Bounders has been a danglers-only establishment since its establishment by Colonel Flashman in the officers' digs at Rawalpindi in the darkest days of the Mutiny.

If the very laws of physics and common sense have somehow altered since then and made necessary some basic realignment in the natural order of things, well then, please do tell us of such wonders, but do not forget to include details of the flying pigs and two-headed talking wonder dogs which attended such a miracle.

I for one would be astounded to hear tales of the same, while you defend this indefensible idea that women should ever set foot within the walls of our beloved Club.

I throw open the floor to discussion.

brisbanetimes.com.au, May 2009

An extraordinary meeting of the Bounders Club

Re: Milky boobs, the public flaunting thereof

Gentlemen, gentlemen, please! Your attention, if I may? Sergeant-at-arms, secure the meeting rooms, would you? And the gin cabinet from Sir Greybeard until proceedings are done?

Gentlemen, as you know, this emergency session of the Bounders has been called in response to the blackguarding of longtime member Lord Koch by a hairy-legged cabal of the most difficult sort of wymyn. Lord Koch it was, of course, who made the perfectly reasonable point that any gent not possessed of a ticket to the better sort of burlesque show most certainly did not want his digestion and repose upset by public confrontation with the determinedly confronting sight of enormously engorged and milk-glistened mammaries for which he has not paid to take a gander.

Sergeant-at-arms, glass of water for Sir Greybeard!

Gentlemen, for having the temerity to give voice only to that which any decent fellow would be thinking, Lord Koch has found himself traduced in the gutter press by the most frightening klatch of harpies and scolds as ever unleashed a savage nag-swarm on a poor chap.

No, no, sit down, Lord Bob, we'll have none of your points of order tonight.

Gentlemen, I had hoped Lord Koch might share with us some idea of what it might be like to find oneself under the concentrated fire of full 20 000 guns of feminazi artillery, but alas on his physician's advice he has repaired to the sherry cellar for the duration. He may be gone some time.

It falls to the gentlemen of the Bounders then to make response to this unwarranted assault on one of our own and we do so sure of our cause and certain of our certainty. I ask you gentlemen to consider the evidence. Evidence that Lord Koch has not been able to put before the baying hounds of public opinion lest they take his arm off while snapping at the proffered offering.

Members of a certain vintage will recall with fond remembrances those days when a fellow was not likely to be assaulted in the peepers by unleashed and milky boobs wherever he went about his business. Not like today when a fellow is not safe to place a bet on the fighting hounds, or climb too quickly into a hansom cab, lest he be brought undone in his endeavours by the unexpected unveiling of grossly distended lady udders spurting forth their contents as some mewling, poorly trained infant attempts to gobble at them like a half-starved Hottentot! Infant screaming, udders gushing, slatternly trollop giving neither fig nor fee for the feelings of the gent thus inconvenienced … it will not stand, gentlemen. It Will Not Stand.

(The minutes of the meeting record only roaring and the stomping of riding boots, leavened by the thud of a wooden leg or two on polished oaken floorboards at this point.)

Gentlemen, gentlemen, please! Some decorum. This is not a common room at Wymyn's College!

I need not point out, but will, that since those happy days of yore the world has not improved one jot. Can it be coincidence, gentlemen, that since this plague of milky boobs unleashed itself in the public realm we have been beset by the most beastly sort of upstarts in the former sandy colonies about the Suez, the decline of the anglophone hegemony and a bothersome infestation of the International Cricket Council by the known associates of the meaner class of subcontinental bookmaker?

Coincidence? I think not!

On a more personal note, I am surely not the only member who has found his previously cherished privileges drastically wound back in the public space because so much of that space is now occupied by squirming, squealing hairless midgets and their ambulatory milk sacks. How many of us, gentlemen, have settled into our first-class seats on the steam train or aero-tube, spread knees to allow the cramped and suffering family jewels some room to breathe, only to find ourselves suddenly slamming said kneecaps together lest they be painted by regurgitated mother's milk from the feeding station next door?

Why, it's enough to make a fellow question his right to adjust the trouser jewels in public at all!

Gentlemen, a crisis is upon us. Lord Koch is the first casualty, but unless we act he will not be the last. I throw open the floor to suggestions as to how we might respond to this modern scourge.

brisbanetimes.com.au, January 2013

An extraordinary meeting of the Bounders Club

Re: Sexy time at the Bounders Club

Cmdr Birmingham (Royal Bermuda Volunteer Naval Reserve, Retired) presiding.

Gentlemen, I have called you here today to discuss a most unusual proposition from the finance committee. As you would know, the books of the Bounders Club are in a parlous state, an unfortunate happenstance I can only sheet home to the ruinous tenure of Mr Brian Waldron as club secretary. The auditors have yet to present their final report, but I'm afraid it appears a good deal of our working capital seems to have been poured down the throats of some of the thirstier Melbourne Storm players.

As such we find ourselves skint, gentlemen. The club's polo stables have already been emptied out and their occupants radically retasked, as you will note if you peruse tonight's menu in the dining room. The bar will be closing early after the meeting, serving its last drinks at 2 am rather than trading through until breakfast.

And I am afraid the crystal has already been hocked to cover our collective losses with the bookmakers. If you will all just keep a hold of your complimentary plastic beaker from the American hamburger clown, you will be entitled to a free refill in the small street-front commissary we have been obliged to lease to him.

None of this is acceptable, gentlemen, but it is unavoidable. For the moment at least.

And so we come to the crux of this meeting, the proposal from the finance committee that in light of our fiscal embarrassment and certain fortuitous societal developments, we might monetise what comparative advantages we do have in an all-out effort to push through and leave this troubling time behind us.

It has come to the attention of committee chair Lord Bob of Nowhere that with the unfortunate liberation of the fairer sex there has come a related, and for us serendipitous, liberation of both their morals and their purse strings.

I shall not beat about the bush, gentlemen. The ladies have to have it and they are willing to pay for it. I presume some of us are still willing to provide it. By way of explanation I table these fascinating accounts in the electronical media of certain ladies coining it like bandits after having set up a pleasure parlour specialising in the provision of Fancy Men for the purpose of pleasuring their lovelorn but cash-rich sisters.

Gentlemen, this is an outrage. I am sure there are any number of you who would be willing to provide this service for free and were circumstances more amenable I would advise you to have at it. But circumstances are not amenable. Circumstances are rather grim, truth be told. So, I propose we adapt a number of the Club's sleeping rooms to receive guests of the female gender, on a strictly paying basis, by the hour, until such a time as our coffers are replenished.

I have no doubt about the popularity of this service should we opt to provide it, but I do wonder who amongst the membership is ready to make the sacrifice for the greater good of the Bounders Club. I, unfortunately, am unable because of The Wound I received at Balaclava. But I can very easily imagine General Havock all trussed up in a fetching array of leather dog collars and fresh underpants, which I am assured the modern sort of lady finds very much to her liking. Or Lord Bob, himself laid out on the chaise longue in the Library, greased from head to toe like an oily whale of love beached on the sands of loneliness and awaiting nought but the heaving, grunting efforts of a well-paying, role-playing lady rescuer to shift him from his precarious situation. There will be others amongst you with your own special bedroom talents, I am sure.

brisbanetimes.com.au, April 2010

The upside of the end of the world

For the true fan of the apocalypse, the end of the world is all about the shooting and shopping. Oh sure, there's the dread horror and the terribly sad bits where everyone dies and you can't get a decent coffee any more. But not everyone dying is a dead loss. Some of them really asked for it, like the scientists who were messing with powers beyond their control and the barista who didn't turn up for work when all I wanted was that one last morning cappuccino, before I fired up the chainsaws duct-taped to my stolen Hilux and cut my way through the screaming hordes standing between me, my last coffee and freedom.

I was disturbed this week then to hear from some guy on the internet that Perth was adjudged to be not just the best place in Australia to see out the end of the world, but one of the best anywhere when the whole world goes down the S-bend. (Archival note for future generations picking over the bones of our dead civilisation: in the early years of the 21st century some guy on the internet replaced 'sources close to the issue', 'high-ranking government officials' and 'many people are now saying' as the gold standard of verification for ridiculous, unverified stories in the mass media.)

I'm not sure why some guy on the internet leaped to the entirely wrongheaded conclusion that Perth was the Big Rock Candy Mountain towards which he'd best point his chainsaw-festooned vehicle when the dead rose or the comets fell. Perhaps he was working from super-secret government plans that somehow leaked before high-ranking government officials opened a massive black bag of wet-work operators to erase the leaks and all who had seen them. I could believe that. Or maybe he was just laying a dummy trail, for dummies to follow into the desert, thereby freeing up precious chainsaws and dwindling cappuccino stocks for those of us who read the tea leaves swirling in the rising sea waters as they poured through the streets of the dying capital and around the buoyant beer kegs I'd bungeed to the Hilux wherever it proved difficult to strap on another chainsaw. I could believe that too. Because I would totally do the same thing.

But I can't believe Perth is a genuine pick to see out the last of days. Not unless you genuinely want them to be *your* last of days.

Most likely the poor judgment call was based on an old io9 story, 'Ten Places to Ride Out the Apocalypse', which listed Perth because of its remote location and vast, agriculturally productive hinterland. What the super-nerds at io9 failed to take into account, of course, is that everyone in WA already rolls around in massive, weaponised 4WDs with circular saws for wheels. *The Cars That Ate Paris* is not a cult Australian autopocalypse flick; it's just a traffic report from the Perth to Mandurah freeway.

No, if you're going to enjoy Armageddon, like anything, you need to prepare. Certain locales will lend themselves more readily to particular cataclysms, and due preparation for the Plague or robot uprising or giant Tasmanian snot-blob invasion (you better believe I added *that* story to the top of my watchlist this week) will see you well placed to enjoy the unparalleled shooting and shopping opportunities. Or shooting and looting, if you're a tedious literalist. (A word of caution. In nine out of ten simulations run in my imagination, tedious literalists are the first to die after scientists messing with powers beyond their control and tardy baristas. They often suffer tragic chainsaw accidents just before the unhinged vicar who has abandoned his faith after God abandoned humanity, and long before the Second Disposable Hottie gets eaten by zombies.)

Brisbane, for instance, has long been recognised by some guy on the internet, who may have been me, as the perfect redoubt against the shambling hordes of the walking dead. Not all of the city, naturally.

Most of the population would have to be sacrificed if only to swell the ranks of the shambling hordes for the hardiest survivors to enjoy. (The hardiest survivors being me, the third-through-sixth Disposable Hotties, the comic relief guy, and some B-list characters who'll hang around long enough for you to become attached to before … you know.) The natural advantages of the subtropical city in any zombie outbreak lie in the many houses that still sit atop high stilts, creating perfect forts once the stairs are cut away – chainsaws aren't just for delinquent java monkeys – and the unusually abundant supplies of rainwater tanks, rooftop solar cells, backyard fruit and veggie patches, and aggressive insect life to nibble away the shuffling Zeds you don't dispose of during a run to the local mall.

Melbourne, on the other hand, is the perfect place to ride out a climate change catastrophe because it would look just like Venice with the waves lapping at the third or fourth floor of Myer on Bourke Street. Unlike Venice, however, the logical grid pattern would make navigating the drowned metropolis less of a chore, especially with a few boatloads of man-eating pirates furiously paddling after you. A few short strokes up to the hilltop fort of the Spring Street cantonment and you're home to the Melbourne Club barracks while flights of arrows rise gracefully from the battlements to feather the carcasses of your cannibal nemeses.

Sydney, of course, can be the only choice for those with an eye for the catastrophic spectacular, as Guillermo del Toro showed us in *Pacific Rim*, and somebody else did in the last telling of *Independence Day*. Nothing says you're having a world-class extinction-level event like destroying the Opera House and the Harbour Bridge. The suburbs of the Upper North Shore too, since del Toro's monster lizards seemed to stomp through them before kicking down the Coat Hanger.

But Perth?

No.

Sun-Herald, February 2014

Ferris Bueller's day of the undead

You know me. I'm Jeanie.

I run the infirmary. And the hydroponic station? I helped set your arm that time you came off the quad bike getting away from Rooney.

Remember?

Jeanie! Jeanie Bueller. Sometimes some of the guys call me Shauna.

...

...

...

(Sigh.)

Yes. I'm Ferris's sister.

No! Don't! I don't want to hear about it. We do not need to 'Save Ferris'. We need to find him and put him down. He's gone. Don't you understand? He thought the rules didn't apply to him. He thought he was special. He thought ... no, he didn't think. He never does. Never did, sorry. He believed he was different to everybody else and he could just do as he damn well pleased.

You know he took the Warthog out with him, don't you? The only safe transport we have. The only way we have of keeping in contact with the other fortresses now that the radio's gone down. Oh, and remind me to tell you about my brother's contribution to that little snafu one day.

He … what?

Well of course I know he's been taking the Warthog out for joyrides with his stupid girlfriend. I'm the one who volunteered to pull the extra shifts in the motor pool when Edson got eaten. I'm the one who ponied up for the fucking minty-fresh blood transfusion you enjoyed after your little quad bike accident and then backed up to do maintenance on the 'hog. Where I was able to check the odometer. Where I was able to confirm what I knew all along, that Ferris and his fucking glove puppet Cameron had been using the Warthog without authorisation.

Three hundred miles they put on the clock. Three hundred and one and seven-tenths to be exact, which I can, because, God help me, somebody has to around here. Three hundred and one point seven miles' worth of gas and hard driving and wear and fucking tear because don't you believe for a moment any of Cameron's bullshit that he sticks to the cleared roads and drives only fast enough to keep ahead of the hunting packs.

Three hundred and one miles. As close to 302 as makes no goddamn difference. In one goddamned day. I will bet you a week's worth of rations they took that thing all the way up to Chicago and back. In one day. Probably drove it around Wrigley Field with half the city shambling after them.

I just … I just don't understand.

I just don't understand why he gets all the breaks and everybody covers for him.

It's his fault that Rooney ended up the way he did, you know. All torn up, dragging half a severed leg behind him and groaning Ferris's name over and over again.

You ever heard of one of them doing that before? Well? No. Me neither. The most you ever get out of them is, 'Braaaaaiiinnnnz.'

But not Mr Rooney. Oh no. He was so intent on finding my brother after the last time he had one of his 'days off' that when one of the cannibal herds was finished with him the last thing anyone saw was his leftovers dragging themselves up the road croaking, 'Ferrrrisssssss.'

So don't tell me … what?

You want what?

…

…

No, I am not giving you any donations for the Save Ferris drive. I've got about three bullets and one half-chewed Twinkie to last me until resupply on Friday and I am deeply fucking disinterested in being told I'm a heartless bitch for not putting in.

Honestly. You people. He will be the death of you. For a little while, anyway, until you reanimate.

My brother is not a hero. My brother is not our saviour. He is a selfish, inconsiderate manchild who perfectly encapsulates the Romney era's solipsistic end-of-the-world view and insatiable appetite for immediate gratification, which, when you think about it, makes him not a thousand miles removed from the creeping hordes of the undead out there on the other side of the Wall. In a nutshell, I hate my brother.

...

...

No, I didn't blow him away, but I will if he tries clawing his way over the Wall. And you wouldn't want to be in my firing line when that happens.

I'm not being a bitch. I don't know why everyone says that about me. I just need you all to understand that everything has changed. We have to grow up. All that crap that Ferris used to go on about, you know, finding the joy in life, because life moves so fast that if you don't stop and look around once in a while you could miss it, well those days are over. They've been over since the day that the dead decided they were missing life too and so they came back for seconds.

We can't afford to live like that any more. There are no days off for anyone. Not now, not ever again … We will never see those days again … and … I'll never see my brother again … I'll never …

What?

He's what? Where?

No. How? I just … I'm speechless. Fucking speechless. How did he get all those sausages from Fromans? Huh? Did anybody think to ask what he was doing, dancing down the trestle tables in the canteen throwing fucking sausages around like party treats? That factory is nearly 150 miles away. It's a fortress, a real fortress. With battlements and boiling oil and everything. Ask yourself, please just ask yourself, how did he get there and back? How did he even get in? Abe Froman doesn't share anything with anyone. Not even the magnificent Ferris Bueller.

I … he, he …

I'll, oh, just forget about it and give me a fucking sausage.

Frankie, 2012

STUFFING YOUR PIEHOLE

Apocalypse pudding

I think we might be doomed. Not by global warming, or terrorism or a fast-mutating dose of bird flu skipping across the species barrier. I think we might be doomed because we're too dumb to live.

My evidence?

If it please the court, I tender a $27 000 pudding.

Or I would, except somebody ate it. After forking out $27 000.

For a pudding.

Okay, it was a nice pudding, made with 28 different types of cocoa, infused with 5 grams of 23-karat 'edible' gold and a bracelet of white diamonds, and you can only buy it in New York, the home of the thousand-dollar white truffle cream-cheese bagel, and celebrity chef Daniel Boulud's altogether more modest $99 hamburger – allegedly the world's most expensive burger, leading me to think that Chef Boulud just isn't trying hard enough. Surely he could swap out the foie gras and black truffle plug at the centre of his organic beef patty with a big lump of oh-so-hard-to-get black-market Russian plutonium. Oozing exclusivity and radiation in equal measure, it would justify plumping out the price a bit more, and keep the meal warm with its gentle bath of radioactive decay.

Stephen Bruce, the restaurateur who came up with the idea for a chocolate pud' that could fund its own ill-advised military adventure in the Middle East, has stepped way up from his previous triumph, the Golden Opulence sundae, for which visiting rock stars and Arabian sheikhs were only too happy to part with a lazy grand.

'It took us a long time to experiment with all the ingredients and flavours, and more than three months were needed just to design the golden spoon,' he told Reuters, which surprises me because last time I checked, gold and diamonds actually have no taste. A crunchy, tooth-cracking mouth-feel to be sure in the case of the rocks, but those big wads of gold leaf that look as though the chef has mistakenly crinkled up the foil from his packet of Winfield Blues on your dessert are gastronomically inert. Odourless, tasteless and incapable of being digested by the human body.

Now, don't get me wrong. I'm a big fan of conspicuous consumption. Up here at the Grotto my Bunnies keep the disco balls in the hovercraft polished to a supernova shine. I like to think it inspires my inferiors to work a little harder, in the hope of one day owning their own stables of bunnies and disco balls. But in doing so I provide a very *public* service.

Unless Mr Bruce's cashed-up gourmands are walking the streets of New York, shovelling mouthfuls of 23-karat gold- and jewel-encrusted chocolate pudding into their dials, you know, just to give the average Joe something to aspire to, then what's the point? All that glitter might look nice on the dessert plate, but in the end it's very, very expensive and literally tasteless.

cheeseburgergothic.com, May 2007

I take it back, soccer

Perhaps I've been a bit hard on the soccer. Perhaps it was wrong of me to make so many cruel jokes about the round ball game, or indeed about the round ball itself, and how much less skill is involved in controlling it than, say, bouncing a Sherrin while twisting through a swarming defence at the MCG, or even through a wobbly, bare-footed defence by a couple of toddlers in the backyard.

Perhaps it was harsh of me to imply that most soccer players are a bunch of hysterical girly-men better suited to amateur theatre, given the way they carry on when they cop a bit of a kick in the shins, or a light trip in the back of play. Not for them the stoic acceptance of blood and pain when some Neanderthal front rower from the South African veldt decides to perform a bit of improvised brain surgery with a set of sharpened steel boot studs. Nope. The merest hint of bodily contact finds someone like David Beckham pirouetting through the air, John Woo style, blubbering for a bandaid and a kiss on the boo boo in the hope of gaining the indulgence of some passing referee.

And maybe, just maybe, it was wrong to imply that soccer fans, at least in this country, are a pack of humourless, thin-skinned munters who have never and will never get over the fact that their beloved sport is a third-order irrelevance because it has never and will never mean anything to a population already in thrall to three other codes.

Yes, maybe that was too harsh.

Because I heard today that soccer fans at the World Cup are going to be forced to drink Budweiser.

The famous American fizzy beverage – it's not actually a beer as defined by Germany's strict centuries-old brewing laws – has been named the official tipple of the 2006 World Cup, after the evil geniuses at the Anheuser-Busch Death Star ponied up 40 million greenbacks for the right to force thirsty Germans to drink their cold, flavorless brew.

Red cheeked, blustering Huns have been pulling on their leather shorts and rushing to the barricades but it is too late. All the oompah bands in all the world will not put Humpty together again. When the first round of the Cup kicks off – that is, about 90 minutes before Australia departs from the tournament in ignominy, again – none of the thousands of top-shelf German lagers or ales, bar one, will be available anywhere within the venues, or indeed within 500 metres of them.

The one exception is Bitburger, a dry, honey-coloured pilsener possessed of exquisite taste and carnivorous lawyers. These latter somehow convinced a judge somewhere, perhaps in a bar, that Budweiser sounded awfully like 'Bitburger' and so they should be allowed to sell their beer at the World Cup too. They'll probably be restricted to a folding card table on the bottom level of the underground car park a mile from the main venue, but the queues will very, very long.

Given the understandable vehemence of the reaction you have to wonder what's in it for Anheuser-Busch. Soccer is even more of a micro-demographic concern in the US, the home of Budweiser, and no amount of marketing tie-in is going to convince a couple of hundred million Euro sceptics that they should give up their tasty hometown brews for a pallid mega McBeer. Indeed, there is a very real risk that forcing them to drink the stuff will simply harden their attitudes against it. After all, 'tis better to be thought of as a shite drink, without opening one's ring pull and confirming the fact beyond all doubt.

If the blog traffic is to be believed – and why the hell shouldn't it be? – American beer lovers are just as bemused by FIFA's decision. Budweiser enjoys a 50 per cent market share in the US, but as the bell curve tells us, 50 per cent of any given population is going to be of below-average intelligence. And the native non-Bud-lovers are torn between horror at the idea of their Ugly American beer giving them an even worse name than they already have on the continent and shameful joy at the idea of forcing it down the German gullet.

Makes you wonder what the Germans ever did to anybody to deserve this.

But not for long.

The Bulletin, June 2006

Save my bacon

If bacon and ham are the new smoking, then smoked ham and bacon must be the new plutonium. But, you know what, if plutonium was as delicious as bacon I'd totally neck a big plate of the stuff. Every day. And so say we all, if the reaction to this week's anti-bacon propaganda is anything to judge by. (And it totally is, because who needs inconvenient science when you have social media snark?)

This so-called International Agency for Research on Cancer and its alleged 800 studies on just how cancertastic certain things are might have impressed the pantywaists at the World Health Organization, but in my Twitter timeline it was all salami and pig meat all the time. Most people quite rightly decided that sure, you might live an extra 20 or 30 years by eating leaves and twigs instead of chocolate-covered bacon rind, but you'd be eating leaves and twigs and not enjoying chocolate-covered bacon rind for the whole time. Excuse me as I state the obvious, but that sounds like hell. What's more, you'd be denying yourself the proven benefits of eating chocolate.

Dialling even further into this voodoo research, the case against red meat comes apart easier than a slow-cooked lamb shoulder. A 17 per cent chance of increased death might sound a little worrying, but let's not forget the flip side – there's an 83 per cent chance of not dying earlier, and a 100 per cent chance of being a lot happier while you weren't dying. That's a statistic that Big Tofu and the vegan conspiracy don't want getting out.

The actual numbers are even more telling. Out of 1000 bacon lovers, 61 are likely to develop bowel cancer. Out of 1000 tofu clowns, 56 will go out backwards *exactly* the same way, probably whining and moaning, 'But I ate all that tofuuuu ...'

If you're genuinely concerned about this, you really don't need to give up everything, all at once. You could wrap two rashers of delicious bacon around your filet mignon instead of three. And you could cook it rare or medium rare, as God intended, rather than burning the goodness out of it. That causes cancer and should be banned. Alternatively, if you absolutely must succumb to these scare campaigns, perhaps I could interest you in a turducken. It doesn't have any bacon, unless you chop up a couple of kilos for the stuffing, but a chicken, pushed into a duck, which sits inside a turkey, is lot more appetising than bean sprouts and smug self-abnegation. And this research proves it is totally not as bad for you as bacon. Not that bacon is bad.

Mmmmm. Bacon.

According to a Dr David Spiegelhalter, 'every bacon sandwich you eat knocks half an hour off your life'. But is half an hour without bacon any kind of life?

The *British Medical Journal* came to its senses and admitted that fat was perfectly good for you, but somehow managed to exclude deliciously fatty bacon sandwiches from this paradigm shift, leading to the dietary fatwa of one Dr David Spiegelhalter.

Even were it true that every bacon butty hastens you towards the grave 30 minutes earlier than might have been the case if you had instead 'enjoyed' some activated walnuts or a nose bag full of alfalfa, does there not come a point where we cry, 'Enough! Just let us have our damn bacon'?

Eggs were once damned as lethal and googy death bombs. Milk was worse than plutonium and Hitler combined. Bread was the staff of life. Now eggs are power-packed little protein hits. Full-cream milk makes you skinnier than skimmed. And bread is dead.

Sure, bacon *probably* isn't as good for you as spinach, but a life spent nibbling through leaf litter will one day end, just as surely and finally as a life wrapped in bacon and drizzled with melted cheese.

Perhaps the secret is not to wrap *everything* in bacon, but not to punish yourself with regret and self-loathing for enjoying the simple pleasures of an occasional BLT, or a burger with the works. Misery kills as surely as bowel cancer.

brisbanetimes.com.au, November 2015

Potato cake terrorist

Ten cents, they cost. Ten cents for a lovely golden medallion of crunchy salty awesome wrapped around a fluffy white heart of perfect potato. It was a 15-minute walk from school, down the hill and through the centre of town, to the Samios family's fish and chippery, but even in the baking, lethal heat of summer it was worth it. For at the end of your trek, nirvana awaited.

Nirvana cost ten cents. And by its name we shall know it.

The potato scallop.

Not, Ms Iselin, if that is your real Australian name, a potato cake. No. What you got for your hard-earned 10-cent piece was a deep-fried potato scallop.

It was ever thus. It will ever be.

I don't know who you are, Iselin. But Iselin sounds a lot like ISIS, and it can't be coincidence that I've managed to mention a death cult determined to undermine our precious Aussie way of life with sharia law, and potato cakes, in the same paragraph. No further proof of how wrong you are is necessary.

I mean, what the fuck even are potato cakes? They sound like something people refuse to eat in the middle of a really bad famine in Poland.

'Jakob. You must eat something. You need your strength. Here. It is not much, I know. Just potato cake scavenged from pile of refuse behind horse rendering factory. But you must ...'

'Gah! Woman, away with you! First you tempt a poor starving fellow with promising smell of rendered horse intestines then you disappoint with filthy potato cake. Be gone before I beat you with my belt.'

'But Jakob, we ate your belt.'

'No potato cakes! They make baby Jesus cry!'

I had never heard of potato cakes before this last, dark and terrible weekend. I would have assumed, if someone had been cruel and unusual enough to offer me one, that they were a small, hard knob of vegan puritanism, fashioned into the shape of a cupcake and baked until everyone just wanted to stab themselves in the brain to escape the wrongness of it all ...

But no! We are somehow to believe that the generations of Aussies who fought off Rommel, fortified by daily airdrops of freshly cooked potato scallops, were actually girding their Aussie loins with an abomination presenting itself in the form of a cake, but secretly containing a deep-fried tuber.

Does that sound like the sort of thing anybody would want to eat?

Cakes are round sweet treats or, in a pinch, lamingtons. They are traditionally baked, not fried, and you never, ever got them from Mr Samios. He was a traditionalist and did not even hold with the modern craze for deep-frying Mars Bars. Mr Samios deep-fried fish and he deep-fried potatoes in the form of chips or scallops.

Mr Samios was a good Australian.

You are no Mr Samios, Ms Iselin.

And the potato scallop will never be a cake.

brisbanetimes.com.au, October 2014

Oh Christmas ham, how did it come to this?

Why does it always come to this between us? How well I recall our early days together. The promise they held. The excitement at just being around you. I said my love for you would never die, Christmas ham, and I spoke the truth as I then felt it. I could speak no other.

And Christmas ham, we were so good together, weren't we? Even now, when everything has gone so wrong between us, I can still recognise that there was a time, there was a place, they mattered and meant that there was love in the world. My love for you, Christmas ham.

Oh yes, I know others said it would not last. Some were even cruel enough to say I was not man enough for you and that you, Christmas ham, were ... well, let's get it out there.

Too big.

But Christmas ham, that did not bother me! Your enormous size was one of the things I loved most about you. Not for me one of those thin little shavings of prosciutto. I like a bit of heft on my Christmas ham,

Christmas ham. There's just so much more for me to love.

And love you I did, Christmas ham. I loved you on toast. I loved you on sandwiches. I loved you on another sandwich because one sandwich full of Christmas ham was barely enough. There were times, Christmas ham, and don't deny it, when my need for you overwhelmed all propriety and I took you and you alone in my mouth. I had to have you inside me, Christmas ham, and if that meant throwing aside even the most modest slice of bread to have at you, then so be it.

Sigh.

But even that was not enough, was it? It never is with you. My devotion is never enough. My hunger is always inadequate.

It started, as it so often does, on Christmas Day. You knew, Christmas ham, you knew that there were other meats coming. You were with me when I picked up rolled pork and both those lamb shoulders. You knew roast chicken is always there and you know what I am like. I've never made any secret of my appetites.

But even though I still had you at the table, you turned, Christmas ham. And you've been on the turn ever since.

I can't even look at you now. The way you insist that everything must be all ham all the time. There are things you can do with a croissant besides putting ham on it, you know. And I've done them, Christmas ham, oh yes I have, I've done them all.

I've even done things with other ham, damn you! You forced me to it.

It wasn't other Christmas ham, no.

It was a cheap and easy store-bought ham sandwich I had when I was out just yesterday. That's right, Christmas ham. I bought ham. From a shop, and I enjoyed it, while you sat there in my fridge, in cold silence.

It's over between us, Christmas ham. I want you out of my fridge now. Just get out and don't come back.

Until next Christmas.

brisbanetimes.com.au, January 2016

Pig night out

A pack of hefty blokes in possession of a good appetite will always be in search of a pork fest. Unconscionably protracted in the planning, painfully abridged in the execution, our night of the suckling pig drew together such a team of these greedy yahoos that its like will ne'er be seen again.

The Night of the Pig was a mission from God. A magnificent obsession. Out there with mad Cap'n Ahab's hunt for the great white whale or the Man of La Mancha's crazed charges against enemy windmills. And *Don Quixote de la Mancha* is no gratuitous classical reference cast like a cultured pearl before you beery swine. Well, actually it is. But it segues really nicely into a consideration of Don Quixote's House of the Suckling Pig, the centre of the pork-loving universe. Familiar to generations of Sydney movie-goers through its cheap, scratchy, Whitlam-era cinema ads.

The Don caught my eye when some pompous twit of a food critic swanned through to nickel and dime the joint to death. As if I give a fuck about the lack of radicchio and tiramisu. For me, the kicker from that review was the clear impression given that these guys could supply you with more pork than you could possibly eat.

Oh baby, I salivated quietly, *racking gut cramps here I come.*

My original plan called for 12 good men and true to repair to the Don's place to stuff themselves insensible on hot, salty pork while drinking so much Mexican beer that someone would accidentally get a tattoo and join the merchant navy. And with but one exception every red-blooded son of Anzac I approached felt as I did, to the universal horror of their girlfriends and heart surgeons, whose eyes bulged at the thought of them gorging on pork until they could gorge no more.

Their neediness was even a little scary. One, a lawyer for a multinational arms conglomerate, suggested hiring a private room where we could eat naked whilst dusky serving wenches scurried hither and yon with tape measures to track the expansion of our waistlines: first to enlarge himself by 20 per cent to win.

As word spread through the city, hopeful pig brothers appeared from all corners wanting a piece of the action. Captain Barnes flew up from Melbourne, avowing that he wouldn't be happy until his fingertips turned grey from restricted blood circulation due to the massive quantities of hog fat congealing in his bloodstream. Sadly we were to be undone by our own appetites.

Meeting in the Century Tavern above Hungry Jack's in George Street, we discovered that despite brave words to the contrary the women in our lives had not organised some counter pig night (or Teste-Fest '98 as one dubbed it). A picnic at Shakespeare in the Park had been mooted. Or a Jane Austen video binge. But despite the tantalising prospect of organising five or six bloke-free hours together at that stupid, interminable *Cloudstreet* play, nothing transpired. After copious hits off the Tooheys Old taps we all agreed this had something to do with girls not being good at sums.

While these weighty deliberations took place, yon editor and photographer inspected the facilities. A couple of thin tweedy college boys – who looked like a good fuck and some pork crackling might be the end of them – they were escorted through the voluminous kitchens by Manuel, who's been with the restaurant for about 300 years. They were introduced to our own specially selected porker, procured from a secret alpine breeding station, the source of the Don's succulent white meat for three decades.

All around them other little piggies lay happily marinating in their trays or slowly roasting in the ovens, a process which can take up to six hours.

Manuel became very excited by the prospect of a magazine review. His only other brush with fame was a cover story in something like *Pig Breeders Monthly*, a long time ago. The details are a little hazy due to the many schooners of Tooheys Old warring with the San Miguels I switched to on arrival, the chewy overbite of a cold San Mig being the only possible consort to such a repast.

With the team finally in place at the bar, our 16 big men blocked all access to and from the body of the restaurant, drawing worried glances from the waitstaff and other diners. The Don's place presented a little like the flagship outlet of an upmarket Alamo-themed restaurant chain: lots of weathered oak and brick and, in the bar, what looked like a couple of wooden cannon bookends untainted by the merest hint of irony. It was the perfect site for an all-male meat fest, but I gotta say we didn't understand all the couples who kept arriving for what were obviously to be romantic dinners. The presence of those few Asian tourists still standing after the regional financial meltdown had sent their tinpot economies back to wholesaling sacks of guano and betel nuts was understandable. They were here by mistake. But surely the locals should know better?

Maybe it had something to do with excellent dating facilities – specifically, the Don's dance floor, on which riotously tipsy thick-waisted hipsters punished the Macarena while Zorro's great-grandson tickled the synth with all the dexterity which his famous forebear deployed in carving his mark into the chests of California's avaricious landowners.

Waiters who hovered with offers of garlic prawns were dismissed to the kitchens with stern orders to start bringing the carcasses and to keep bringing them until our corrupt and bloated bodies lay groaning on the floor, covered in a thick greasy sheen of glistening lard and faintly creaking as the monstrous volume of meat pressed against straining ribs and taut belly skin.

I don't think they knew what they were dealing with.

Piles of warm crusty bread rolls arrived but any of the eager juveniles who reached for them were quickly smacked back into line. A big trap for young players. Save space for the pig. The first pig which arrived was laid on the table and I do not exaggerate when I say that its bones had been sucked clean before the somewhat superfluous vegetables arrived 2 minutes later.

It was around about this point that Manuel, who had previously been the very picture of a genial host, became worried.

'More pig! More pig!' we cried. More plates arrived and were cleaned off with ferociously efficient despatch. 'Ha ha,' laughed Manuel nervously. 'We normally get romantic couple in here. They don't eat so much.'

'More pig! More pig!' we cried.

The waiters eyed each other anxiously and began to back away from the table. The horrible truth started to dawn on me. A special alpine breeding station. Six-hour cooking time. A restaurant full of diners all tucking into their meals while we denuded the bar.

Oh. My. Fucking. God.

They were short of pig. Or, more likely, they had enough pig for a normal night but this was most assuredly not a normal night.

All joking aside, Manuel,' muttered Robbie, 'where's the rest of the pig, man?'

The staff were sweating by now. We suggested they might care to scrape the plates of the other diners whose eyes had proven too big for their bellies. I don't know whether they did this but we were about to do it ourselves when a few more plates turned up.

And in defence of the Don let me say that this was magnificent pig. The best any of us had ever tasted. So keen was Adam Spencer for a few more scraps of its golden goodness that he and Barnes picked clean the skull of the first beast Manuel had laid before us. Eyeballs and all.

But ... they were short of pig. We had broken them.

As we spilled out onto George Street a raucous

argument broke out over whether we should head back to the Century to drown our sorrows and fill the empty spaces in our pig-loving hearts with Tooheys Old, or whether we should go to Hungry Jack's first.

I think you all know which option we chose.

cheeseburgergothic.com, August 1998

Grand theft mango

Wasn't me what stole no giant mango. I dunno who's got the thing. I just know it wasn't me what nicked it, guvnor. I mighta done a few things in me time, but I never trousered no giant mango, sir.

Not that I couldn't if I wanted to, right? Cos my pants, they're utterly voluminous, guv. They have to be on account of the exceptionally large trouser equipment I am forced by good luck and the magic of the Birmingham family DNA to carry through this life. We all have our burdens, sir, and my particular burden is sausage shaped and spectacularly oversized.

But I promise you, I did not take no giant mango.

I know! I know I got form, guvnor. I know you got me for making off with that giant KFC bucket on top of the pole during that university scavenger hunt. But I brought it right back, didn't I, but? Just as soon as I ascertained that there was no actual fried chicken in said revolving bucket. Just as soon as I lodged my complaint with the authorities about the blatantly misleading and deceptive conduct of one Sanders, comma,

Colonel, full stop, as regards the finger-fuckin'-lickin' goodness to be obtained upon his premises of business, and by implications there upon, from his big rotating bucket what was on the pole enticing me in, guv. A disgrace was what that was, I tell you, sir, an absolute disgrace, and I should have been applauded for exposing the fraud upon the community by this Sanders hoodlum, not harassed by your constables in the first instance and the magistrates in the second.

And yes, admitted without prejudice, I am the one what erected, as a simple prank and jolly jape, sir, that gigantic novelty penis, not my own, in the middle of the university senate garden party that one time when we all had a good larf about it. But I would point out that contrary to the modus operandi of the villains what done this particular job with the Giant Mango of the good town of Bowen, that I *added* that enormous phallus to the scenery, rather than subtracting it therefrom, and not in my usual fashion either, with a loosening of the belt and dropping of the strides I did.

So, no, guvnor, I am not the cove what you are lookin' for in this particular instance.

If you are serious about doing your job here, Mister Plod, and not simply 'arassing an honest scribbler what is going about the business of his various pursuits, you might like to 'ave a word with one Newman, comma, Campbell, full stop.

As I understand it he 'as recently 'ad purloined from his very person a goodly number of precious votes, and he is just the sort of cove what I would expect to be making off with an honest punter's giant mango to either soothe and succour his own hurtful feelings of rejection, or more likely, to entice others, Colonel Sanders-style, with false promises of sweet-ness and tasty treats should they just follow him up this dark alley and lean over this 'ere empty ballot box.

brisbanetimes.com.au, February 2014

WORK IT, BITCH

The meeting

I called a meeting this week. I felt it was important to meet because I read an article in the *Wall Street Journal* about how checklists could turn ineffective meetings into growling, super-charged engines of productivity. My spluttering, lawnmower engine of productivity often coughs and stalls when I'm distracted by articles of eye-glazing dullness on sites I would never visit in a million years were I not on deadline, so at the top of my meeting checklist was an agenda item to discuss the importance of not reading *Wall Street Journal* articles about meeting checklists.

I summoned my department heads and senior VPs of this and that, which, since I work from home, meant the cat and the dog. The dog, who is the hero of our organisation's long struggle to waste as little effort as possible was already efficiently asleep under my desk, her early arrival at the meeting signalled by gentle farts and a rumbling snore.

The cat, however, was nowhere to be seen. This meeting was already going off the rails. Not sure how to proceed, I checked back with the *Journal*.

The 'first thing to check', said the *Wall Street Journal*, was whether this meeting required 'a meeting' or whether we could simply meet. Given the many long-festering rivalries between my subordinates, disputes which have on occasion erupted into open hostilities, the chances of being able to resolve anything during some informal corridor meet-up were judged to be somewhat less than the chances of any such meet-up turning into a yowling, spitting explosion of bad blood and fur.

It seemed then that we did require a proper meeting, because important working people in this go-go business world of ours are always meeting, and if we were not to be left behind it was time to get down to business and start checking off that list. Cat or no cat.

The dog farted, once, softly in agreement.

Having satisfied the need for our meeting, but still hamstrung by the absence of a key player, I turned to the *Journal* for guidance. The dog lifted her head at the mention of ham.

Are the right people meeting, the *Journal* demanded to know, and only the right people? The dog signalled her agreement with some on-topic flatulence that, as far as she was concerned, we had everyone present who needed to be present, but there should probably be some ham, too. I opened a window to clear the air of her contribution. She did have a point, though. According to the *Wall Street Journal*, anyone not directly contributing to the meeting was nothing more than a Meeting Tourist and should be detailed off to more productive work.

This raised an important point that I felt justified moving off-agenda, even if only briefly, lest this meeting fail to meet its objectives, forcing me to return to writing something for money. The cat, by his studied indifference to and absence from a meeting he very well knew to be important to the future of this whole operation, was not contributing. As such he really couldn't be considered anything more than a Meeting Tourist and should be dismissed to get back to his core competencies of having a long nap on the front deck unless he was already busy sleeping in the sunny spot on the couch.

But if the cat wasn't there, how could we even move these things forward?

Well, *Wall Street Journal*? Well?!!?

The *Journal*, never one to be taken unexpectedly by the unexpected, demanded to know, 'Who is leading this meeting?' For the first time I was actually thankful for the absence of the cat, which has long questioned and even openly challenged the formal hierarchy of our organisation.

'Me,' I said. 'I'm in charge here. Don't listen to the cat.'

I could have sworn the dog laughed at that point, but she cunningly pretended to be asleep again and turned it into a snore when I glared at her. This whole meeting was teetering precariously on the edge of collapse and ignominy. I had deadlines to attend to, paying deadlines, and yet here I was stuck in some interminable meeting that stopped me from moving onto other things which could have just as unprofitably stopped me from moving onto those deadlines.

BuzzFeed's very important articles on 'The Miniature Pigs You Need to See Before You Die' and '40 Things We Learned at the Hedgehog Convention' remained unread while I was shitting stress kittens trying to deal with the ticking timebomb of this whole meeting checklist fucktrosity.

The last thing I needed to hear at that moment was the whiny, judgmental drone of the *Wall Street Fucking Journal* asking, 'Are you stressing yourself by trying to run the agenda, keep time, take notes, direct the conversation all at once?'

No! I was stressing myself by trying to bring some semblance of order to a shambles of a day that had been torpedoed amidships by my shiftless and disloyal feline Vice President for Lounging Around on His Furry Arse All Day and the complete lack of anything even resembling support from Farty the

Wonder Dog, who decided to opt out of any sensible contribution just because there was no ham on the agenda.

Finally, in a fit of rage I declared the meeting closed and stormed out of the office, only to be confronted by the cat, arriving late, saying he'd heard there was ham.

Sydney Morning Herald, July 2013

Procrastination masterclass

Good morning. Oh, wait. Yes. Sorry. I meant good afternoon. And welcome to the Procrastination Masterclass. I'd like to thank those of you who made the effort to get here and ask you what you thought you were doing putting in all that effort when you could have been catching up on all the *House of Cards* episodes you haven't watched yet. Shame on you.

I'm JB and I will be your master for today's class. You might know me from some of the very interesting articles I failed to submit on time, or the amusing columns I never got around to writing at all. I have not published more than a dozen books which I'm sure would have been very popular, and some of which were undoubtedly a lay-down misère to not win some quite prestigious awards had they been written, which they weren't.

Some very famous writers are quite famously not very good at procrastinating. Stephen King's work ethic is so strong that he was able to turn in manuscripts even at his lowest ebb as a drunken coke-addled wastrel, and he was hit by a car and run over! Congratulations on taking the first steps out of the path of the on-rushing car that might have run you over had you not decided to take my class. I have all of your home addresses from the enrolment forms, so it was a very real possibility.

By the end of this class you will be qualified to say that you have attended my class, and you will not have been run over. To streamline the mastering process I will now dot-point the following points I wish to cover.

Must write out dot-point list

That's as far as I was able to get before Netflix released *Stranger Things* in binge-ready format. Please note that I do intend to get around to watching it after I've flicked through the new *Star Trek* comic where all of the original *Enterprise* crew are chicks, except for the chicks who are now guys.

I do have a PowerPoint, however. It is unrelated to the topic and a small child still in primary school made it for me, so it's not very good. But it does have some very funny pictures from the internet. Let's spend an hour looking at that.

...

Welcome back, and as for the dot-point rundown of today's class, I would strongly suggest you take notes, unless you've already moved on to doodling flip-book pictures of exploding German tanks in the corner of your new Moleskine notebook. In which case, props to you and there will be extra credit if your explosions are in colour. I will review your work, the night before my next newspaper column is due, but you are almost certainly ready to graduate to my Advanced Masterclass on choosing the right pen for your new Moleskine notebook. Four out of five writers in cafes haven't taken this class, which goes to show how advanced and elite it is. The other one out of those five would have totally taken the class but may have lost the initial email alerting them to it, and then accidentally blocked all my subsequent marketing emails.

I see from the excruciatingly slow sweep of the minute hand and the ticking of the overloud clock at the back of the room that we haven't even started the actual class yet, which means it's time for coffee. Or breakfast gin, for those full-time professional writers among us. Breakfast is the most important meal for the professional writer, commanding the approaches to morning-tea time, as it does, and thus being strategically placed to flow naturally into lunch and dinner. And a professional writer sans breakfast gin is little better than a blogger.

Allow me at this point to make my apologies to all the bloggers who have enrolled for today's Masterclass and paid upfront. Your money is very important to me. Even more so now that it's become my money.

There will be a module dealing specifically with the challenges of online time-wasting for online writing professionals such as yourselves. It is scheduled to be available in the second half of 2017 and I look forward to seeing more of your money when I actually run the class in 2019.

In the meantime, I encourage you all to follow me on Twitter, which allows me to segue into talking about Twitter. Arguably there is no more powerful tool in the hands of the master procrastinator than this premier microblogging service because the guy who invented Flappy Bird took it off the App Store. I don't propose to discuss the relative merits of Twitter versus Facebook because I can get another seminar out of that, and if I use the words 'premium' and 'marketing' and 'brand', and I call myself a ninja, I can charge even more for it.

I can see we're coming to the end of the Masterclass column, however, and before we get anything done I'd like to return to the topic of that *Star Trek* comic, because it seems to me there's something wrong when all the sexy *Star Trek* ladies (like Captain Jane Kirk, geddit?) are wearing pants, which isn't true to the original series at all and probably deserves a blog entry. I will write that blog entry. Tomorrow.

Sun-Herald, February 2014

I am from the Microsoft Security

The phone rings. It rings about the same time most days. Four in the afternoon for me; 11.30 am in Kolkata. Just enough time before a yummy lamb korma lunch for the ever-helpful mavens of the Microsoft Security to secure my security from the many, many security threats that I, a helpless Apple slave with no Microsoft products in my house (save for an Xbox), will never face.

'Hello, am I speaking to owner of the house, because I am the Microsoft Security and your computer is to be showing up on our systems as being very insecure, sir or madam.'

A scammer!

This could go one of two ways.

With a book, a column or a feature article deadline pressing in, I might just hang up.

More likely though, some editor or publisher will have to chew their fingernails down that little bit further, because, damn it, I have the Microsoft Security on the line and I am to be showing up on their systems as being very insecure.

'Oh, oh dear, yes. You are. You are speaking to the owner of the house. What seems to be the problem, Microsoft Security? Is it my windows? Is someone coming in through my windows? Can you see that from there?'

A pause, a breath catching on the line so many thousands of miles away. Could it be this easy? The training supervisor emphasised the arrogance of the Germans, the helpful naivety of the Americans and the drunken stupidity of the Australians. Could this one be drunk already? The little onscreen world clock display shows it to be late in the afternoon in Australia. The entire country could already be in a shameful spiral of alcohol abuse. Best to strike now and get that credit card number before this drunken convict cannot summon the sense to remember it or even the manual dexterity to pull the card from his wallet with fat, numb fingers.

'No sir, yes sir, there is no one at your window. It is your Windows computer that is being attacked, sir. The Microsoft Windows Security shows me you have many, many of the viruses and I am authorised to remove them for you, sir.'

'Oh, thank God. But how did they get on my computer?'

'Oh, there are many ways to trick an honest Microsoft user, sir.'

If a top operative of the Microsoft Security would ever be so puffed up with the pleasure of his own cunning as to smirk at a poor drunken convict from the Antipodes, I am certain I can sense that smirk right now, across the vast oceans of distance that separate us. Time to puncture it.

'Is it the pornography?' I ask.

'Excuse me, sir?'

'The pornography. Is that where I got my viruses? Are they infecting my pornography?'

Yes. It appears the Australian has been drinking.

'Er, it is possible, sir. If you could help me now I will just ...'

'Because I watch a lot of pornography on my computer, you know. It's pretty much all I do. All day. In fact I'm watching pornography right now. Quite a lot, actually. I have many open windows all with pornography in them. Oh my God, do they all have the virus? Can you tell on your system? Can you see my pornography? Is it infected?'

'No, sir. Your pornography is not the issue, sir. Please, sir, if you could just help me. Perhaps by closing the windows with the pornography and focusing on what we have to do, sir.'

'All of the windows, you mean? Because they all have pornography in them. Even the word processor.'

In a curious gender difference, at this point almost

every female employee of the Microsoft Security hangs up. But the men plug on. It takes them about 10 minutes to get me to close all my pornography windows because by now I've started a stopwatch on my iPhone and I make sure it takes them 10 minutes.

'So the pornography is gone, sir?'

'I'm afraid so. But I have magazines.'

'Put down the magazines, sir.'

'Are they infected too?'

'No, sir, but we need to get on with this.'

'Okay. What next?'

'We need to run a diagnostic, sir. Can you follow instructions? Will you do as I ask, sir?'

'Of course. What do I do?'

It gets tricky here. The helpful man from the Microsoft Security begins issuing instructions for me to do things that, on a Windows computer, would presumably allow him to take control of the machine and begin making merry with the files and apps, cracking open email, for instance, and hoovering up all the contents to be scanned later for credit card numbers, login details to online banking and so forth.

'Sorry, sorry,' I say. 'I might have to restart the computer.'

'But why, sir? We are not up to that part.'

'I got some drool in the keys. There's a bit of smoke.'

Unfortunately, never having owned a Windows machine, I cannot follow the Microsoft Security's exact instructions, so I must rely on cunning and subterfuge. Cunning and subterfuge and the belief of at least one Indian scam caller that Australians are not just stupid drunks but wretched, drooling perverts too.

'Have you gone to website address I gave you, sir?'

'Er, I tried to.'

'What do you mean you tried?'

'Well, I typed it in the address bar thingy.'

'And what is onscreen, sir?'

'Pornography.'

A pause.

'What?'

'Pornography. I think it's Russian. Does that help?'

A sigh.

'No, sir.'

And so we begin again. Or he hangs up, cursing me as an Aussie smart-arse. Just under an hour is my record. An hour in which I got no paying work done, but of course neither did he.

Sun-Herald, February 2014

There will be typos

It was kind of you not to point out the embarrassing typo in the subject line of the very first edition of *Alien Side Boob*. I don't know how it could have 'happned', but it was inevitable that I wouldn't notice until half a second after hitting send.

It was not my worst typo.

Many years ago, when working for the defence department, vetting applicants for high-level security clearances, I miswrote of a perfectly acceptable army colonel: 'He should not be cleared.'

Luckily, for the defence of the nation and his career, he was eventually cleared, no thanks to my fumbly bacon tongs inserting that unwanted 'not' into the colonel's personnel file.

I have some sympathy then for that poor bastard running IT security for the Clinton campaign during the recent election: the guy who got tumbled out of bed at ohfuckno-thirty in the AM to vet a phishing email from Vladimir Putin, the guy who, half asleep and bleary-eyed, replied to Clinton's campaign director that Putin's email was cool, rather than 'not cool'.

It happens.

It famously happened to the King James Bible when the printers updated the Ten Commandments for the go-go fun times of the 1630s with the fashion-forward edict, 'Thou shalt commit adultery.'

It could even happen to you this very day, so be kind when you come across some poor soul burning in Typo Hell. You are all one autocorrect away from telling your very important New York publisher that you've returned an edited manuscript via FedEx, enthusiastically texting them, 'Yes. I've sent you a faecal package!'

(And, yes. That was me, giving succour to those critics who've long insisted that my books are shit.)

If you're tempted to point and jeer at others' typographic misfortune, perhaps you should walk a mile in the shoes of the *Washington Post* social listings reporter who, rather than informing readers that President Wilson had been 'entertaining' his wife-to-be, Edith, wrote instead that he had been 'entering' her.

Recall too the venerable *Times* of London once wrote of Queen Victoria crossing a newly built bridge, 'THE QUEEN HERSELF PISSED GRACIOUSLY OVER THE MAGNIFICENT EDIFICE.'

I had to use all-caps there, because of course

the *Times* did not just hide this somewhat surprising disclosure in a small paragraph at the end of the story. It screamed the news from the headline.

If you do find yourself denying somebody their Top Secret clearance today, or misspelling the name of the company you just sent your CV and job application to, try to pull yourself out of the shame spiral. At least you didn't bankrupt anyone, unlike the guy at a Roswell, New Mexico, car dealership in 2007. He had a cunning plan to mail out 50 000 scratchies, one of which would have a $1000 cash prize. Greasy corndog fingers and a lack of attention to detail at the direct marketing company scattered 50 000 golden tickets all over Roswell, putting the dealership on the hook for $50 million.

That was micro-beer compared to the $225 million lost by Japan's Mizuho Securities in 2005, when they floated a stock offer at significantly less than the five grand a share intended. The first typo entered into the Tokyo Stock Exchange computer system dropped the share price to one yen. A fraction of a cent. Not content with this egregious up-fucking, Mizuho doubled down, a second typo putting *forty times* the number of shares they were supposed to offer onto the market. At the ruinous discount of one-tenth of 1 per cent of fuck all. The Tokyo Stock Exchange does not allow replays. The only concession made to Mizuho execs was a chance to wash their hands before choosing an appropriate *seppuku* blade.

Still, as bad as that was for those guys, we've all suffered much worse from the 147-year-old typo in a German scientific paper that overstated the iron content of spinach by 1000 per cent.

Bottom line, Popeye lied.

The government's nutritional standards are bullshit.

And your mother cannot be trusted.

Spinach will not make you strong. It will just stick to your teeth and make you look like a trash Santa who forgot to run a twig over his rotten choppers after climbing out of the dumpster in the morning.

Take that happy thought into the day with you.

I'll be back on Friday.

Until then, in God we thrust.

aliensideboob.com, January 2017

SPORTS AND LEISURE

Licence to drink

Thank goodness that common sense has finally won a gold medal. Granted, it's only a Commonwealth gold, but common sense is confident it can build on that performance and take Australia all the way at the Olympics too.

And where did common sense triumph? In the pool? At the track and field? On the green at the lawn bowls? No, this was a victory for common sense everywhere. In the blood-spattered boxing ring, on the blood-spattered judo mat, at the blood-drenched shooting range, because common sense has decreed that Aussie athletes can still compete while enjoying their sacred birthright to get on the turps before stumbling out, bleary-eyed and rough-headed, to give the world a bloody good hiding, mate.

At the Glasgow Commonwealth Games (now forever known as the Common Sense Games) the weights are off. The taps are open. The Australian team has been given a licence to drink.

This has been a long time coming. There can be

no doubt that the decline in our power as the world's sporting powerhouse coincides directly with the rise of so-called health and fitness professionals. Ha! Professional bullshitters maybe, with undeclared interests in activated almond factories, coconut water processing plants, and death camps disguised as yoga retreats.

Did Dougie Walters score a century between tea and stumps in the 1974–75 Ashes series on tofu shakes and goji berries? The hell he did. His preparation to take apart the English seamers consisted of sucking down two packets of unfiltered, lethally dangerous high-tar cigarettes and a carton of Tooheys Old, plus another carton of Tooheys Old in the drinks break. He didn't warm up with yoga or Pilates; he warmed up by flogging the hide off Bob Willis.

The Organising Committee of the Commonwealth Games are to be applauded for organising drinks in Glasgow, and thin-lipped naysayers be damned. The Scots are universally known as a quiet, abstemious people, and Glasgow a centre of high culture and refinement. No ill will come of this, of that we can be sure.

Australian chef de mission Steve Moneghetti has stated that the team agreement 'pretty clearly sets out that your behaviour as a representative of the Australian Commonwealth Games team is expected to be at a high level'. There will be no sneaking out on your shout, no wimping it with soft drinks or mineral water, and everybody will be kicking in for the food whether they had half a dozen haggis and bacon burgers or a single slice of that stupid vegetarian pizza some buzz-killing idiot ordered.

In a sign that Australian sport might finally be growing up, Moneghetti has promised that any problems will be dealt with quietly and maturely. 'If we need to have a chat, or grab a couple of athletes and have a word to them, we'll do that,' he said. No chance in Glasgow, then, that we'll be embarrassed by reports of some piker in the Rugby Sevens refusing to kick on after the bell is run for last drinks. A team elder, some venerated sporting legend like Warwick Todd, will be there to make sure everybody piles into a couple taxis and makes it to this all-night tranny bar they heard about.

Australia will not be embarrassed. This being the Commonwealth Games, however, the rest of the world will be. Canada most of all, but England too, now all their Olympic lolly has run out and the natural order of things has resumed. Do not be surprised if, far from looking askance at Australia's new drinking policy, our traditional victims at the Games insist on it. It's not beyond the realm of the possible that late rule changes will make it compulsory for antipodean athletes to get an absolute skinful before turning up.

Well, let them. Little do they understand the sleeping, badly hungover giant they have awakened. For as sweet as the long, difficult climb to the victor's podium might be, it is all the sweeter for doing so with a six-pack in one hand and a haggis and bacon burger in the other.

smh.com.au, July 2014

Eating his way to the top

'Luis Suárez's alleged bite on Italy defender Giorgio Chiellini has cast a pall on the 2014 World Cup,' reports the ABC.

Seriously? Luis Suárez chomps on a dude and it 'casts a pall' on the whole World Cup? It was just a little nibble, after all. It's not like he took a leg off Chiellini. And it was nothing like the bite the hooligans of FIFA took out of poor old Brazil when they were shaking them down for the 'privilege' of hosting the World Cup in the first place, a privilege which cost the impoverished South American nation such a grotesque sum of money it didn't really have that even Brazilians who were clinically insane with lust for the beautiful game rioted in their unpaved streets.

The thousands of indentured slaves – sorry, should I say 'construction workers'? – who'll die building Qatar's opulent World Cup stadium for 2022 might arguably be a little miffed that Luis 'Chompy' Suárez gets to cast a pall over the Cup, while their inevitable deaths will be more like background colour. Indeed, given the chance, many of them would undoubtedly tuck in for a bit of Italian with Suárez if it meant they could support their impoverished families as well as the Uruguayan cannibal can look after his. Assuming he didn't eat them on his way to the top.

There's a good deal of inconsistency here. Hypocrisy, even. We normally applaud and support scrappy underdogs like Suárez who get hold of a bone and won't let go, whether it's a shot at glory with an international super club like Liverpool, or the tasty, tasty femur of an opposing midfielder. Was Mike Tyson pilloried for making finger food of Evander Holyfield's earlobe? Well, yes, he was, but surely only because of the equity issue. It was hardly fair for Tyson to load up on such a rich source of protein during the bout while offering nothing to sustain Holyfield beyond a savage storm of uppercuts to keep him from falling to the canvas with blood loss.

Just as everyone knew Qatar would have to pay out millions in bribes to secure the Cup in 2022, we were all surely just waiting for the moment someone would have to pay in blood, and perhaps a little gristle, for letting Suárez into the World Cup in 2014. Was nobody paying attention back in October 2011, when he sank his fangs into PSV Eindhoven's Otman Bakkal? Okay, granted, the ref wasn't, but the match review committee were, and he got a seven-match ban during which to digest his tucker.

If the ban was meant to make him think it over, it succeeded. After due consideration Suárez thought he was feeling rather peckish and would like another course, thank you very much. This time it was Chelsea defender Branislav Ivanović who was taken up into the food chain. Contending with the Liverpool striker in the penalty area, Ivanović was clearly horrified to discover the Uruguayan hungering for red meat over football glory as he looked down and found those famous choppers sunk into his forearm.

Perhaps it's the Latin tapas culture that's to blame? Tasty little dishes, to be sure, but never enough to leave a man feeling sated, not when he does the hard work of running up and down a field after a soccer ball for millions of dollars. It's Suárez I feel sorry for in all this. Should he miss the showdown against Germany, as one fan on Twitter pointed out, he'll be utterly devastated. 'Apparently he quite fancied a shoulder of Lahm ...'

abc.net.au, June 2014

The Sydney to Hobart Yacht Race is a naval battle in the never-ending class war

All cultures have their mysteries. Ghost stories, like the Roanoke Colony of early America. Mute artefacts like the silent stone guardians of Easter Island. Australia is no different. We have our own brush with the transcendent and the incomprehensible at this time every year. It is the Sydney to Hobart Yacht Race.

Seriously, Australia, why is this still even a thing?

Have we nothing better to do than watch arrogant millionaires at play? That's why we invented Rugby League.

The reasons for our original enthralment by this annual festival of damp, fathomless tedium and puzzling arcana are not hard to winkle out. It is rooted in the lethal boredom of the old summertime non-ratings period on the telly when, bloated with leftover pork and still drunk from toasting the birth of Santa with a hundred and eleventy Christmas Day beers, we desperately searched all four free-to-air channels for something to watch. And there was the boat race, because billionaires love boat races, and by a happy coincidence they also tend to own TV stations which could broadcast them having fun on the water.

When your only alternative was watching Bill Lawry talk up the rain forecast from the Boxing Day Test, a couple of hours dozing fitfully on the couch with vague dreams of Harbourside breezes was a reasonable way to wait for your grossly distended belly to return to something like its normal circumference.

This is no longer the case.

We are never more than a click away from an infinite stream of much better entertainment than whatever the hell a tacking duel is. And most of us actually have no excuse for not hitting those streams, given how far behind we've fallen with *The Walking Dead* and *Orange Is the New Black*. Those TV shows aren't going to binge themselves, people!

If you are some sort of freak and the idea of physical activity appeals, don't just sit there and watch a bunch of billionaires' minions running from one side of a grotesquely expensive superyacht to another. You can get yourself down to the Boxing Day sales for an even more vigorous workout. The billionaires won't care, honest. They already own everything and will wholeheartedly approve of your going deeper into unsustainable debt to increase the value of their gargantuan fortunes by mindlessly shopping for even more crap you don't need, with money you don't have.

But it's a tradition of heritage, you protest. We always watch the Sydney to Hobart.

No you don't. You just think you do because it is inescapable, like death and taxes. Unless you're a billionaire yacht owner, of course, in which case the tax system exists merely to channel the few remaining pennies out of the grubby paws of the lumpenproles and onto your giant Scrooge McDuck–style mountain o' doubloons, the billionaire version of a small-change jar, from which to cover the operating costs of their ridiculous superyachts.

But JB, they're not all billionaires, I hear you protest, probably because you're the paid lackey of a billionaire. Well fair point, they're not. In any Sydney to Hobart Yacht Race there will be at least one crew of gallant little street urchins or amputees or reformed and genuinely penitent torturers from the former Romanian intelligence directorate, all of them lathered with 50-plus sunscreen and fleeting media attention to provide a heartwarming distraction from the aquatic pig circus. And good for them. But don't imagine we'd all be following their antics with slavish devotion if they decided the morning after Christmas to wander on down to the harbour for a bit of a bash about in a borrowed tinny.

We suffer this event every year because it reminds

us of our place in the world. Facedown in the bilge water, while the rich guys lord it over us up in the sun.

The New Daily, December 2016

The Biggest Loser recap: appetite for reduction

We gorged on a combination of fat, tears and humiliation; now it's time for regurgitation, Biggest Loser—*style.*

The glittery curtain goes up at Ten's RSL Night-club of Our Dreams and Hopes, the golden spotlights spear down through the darkness of a nation's wanton appetites and collective self-loathing, aaaand it's Hayley! Looking fabulous! And beaming, just beaming, to be back for another *Biggest Loser* finale.

Unlike Tiffany.

Who's … er … not … this year.

But never mind. The crowd erupts into cheers and applause, the stirring strings of the Channel Ten Big Band bestir themselves and 5000 kilos of unsightly human jello are montaged away in mere seconds. Eight years of dummy spits, tantrums and foot stamping, and that just from the trainers. The baby goat bleating of last year's mummy's boy. The first snarl of Michelle Bridges directing traffic 'down Pussy Street or Man Up Road'. The first inappropriate tweet to reference Michelle's unfortunate 'Pussy Street' sound bite in the context of the rumours about her and Commando.

And whimpering. Lots and lots of whimpering.

We come for the bullying and humiliation, but we stay for the whimpering. And the cruel, cruel laughter.

Perhaps we even hang around for the occasional inspiration, whether real and touching in a sweaty, kind of off-putting way, or manufactured by the producers in cringeworthy stunts like *TBL* 2013's 'Promise' motif.

'My promise is to find the happy person that is hiding within me.'

And my promise is not to make obvious jokes about how many people could happily hide inside some of these guys, or point out that it's the happy person 'who' is hiding in there, not the happy person 'that'.

Because looking hot is important, but so is using the right word.

For eight years we have gathered once a year on our couches and recliner rockers to watch and to judge Ten's chubby warriors, to cheer on our favourites, to boo the villain, and to push handfuls of deep dish pizza and chicken nuggets into all of our head holes without even bothering to remove the irony first.

For eight years we have led the global fat TV franchise, delivering up the world's biggest contestant since that last one, who was also ours.

'Big Kev,' roared Shannon in flashback, 'was about to redefine himself.' And he did, as an eliminated contestant in one of the very early rounds. Oh those early days, how could we forget them? The crying. The vomiting. The treadmill comedy and climbing-net pratfalls. Well, just in case we did – or in case, like many of tonight's viewers, we only popped in at the very end to watch the holograms do the walk of shame in their undies next to their much-reduced, or some-what-reduced, or just cunningly wardrobed selves – the entire season, it transpires, can be compressed into 12 seconds of vision. Everything else was just filler and KFC ads.

But the kilos dropped. The fists pumped. And the tatts were out on proud display. The first question that arises as the weigh-in montage kicks off is, 'Was this the most-tattooed *Biggest Loser* series of all?' The ink was everywhere. On man boobs, love handles, ankles, arms, butt cracks, bingo wings, back flaps, the lot. Enough to wonder whether outlawing tattoo parlours might be an unusual but effective response to the national obesity crisis. Not the fancy tattoo specialists who do Shan-non's and Commando's ink, just the cheap ones that are probably luring clients in with free fried chicken and old fried chicken barrels full of free Coke.

But enough of this side-questy search for mean-ing. Everyone suddenly looks happier, and marginally thinner, and the music is suddenly upbeat so we must believe the voice-over man when he tells us that the contestants grew stronger and faster and more and more awesomer. We need not trust him when he tells us they went on to form the greatest league of crime fighters the world has ever known, because he doesn't, in spite of how much we all secretly want him to say that.

Three teams did go on further than all the others, however, and helpfully they represent useful archetypes we might all invest in. Gerald and Todd, everyone's favourites, fighting for the money to pay their daughter/sister's hospital bills. King Richard and Princess Amber, fighting to extend the King's tyrannical rule over the $200 000 prize money. And Katie and Robyn, the orange girls? Fighting for a clue.

Who will be crowned Australia's Biggest Losers?

Dunno yet, because it's time for one last Cyndi Lauper cover. One last series of Instagrammed shots of sweating, worn-out fat people looking like they wish they'd actually been shot rather than signed up for this deep level of hell.

Then Hayley's back onstage at the RSL, and the audience is clapping and cheering but looking a little anxious as the cold, judgmental eye of the camera sweeps over them, because more than a few could also have manned up and got the hell out of the all-you-can-eat buffet in Pussy Street 12 weeks ago. That's the shameful secret of *Biggest Loser*. It invites us to judge ourselves.

But mostly others.

Judge them for their fat, for their weakness, for their failures physical and emotional. For their failures as parents, friends, children and partners.

Which means it must be time for conflict! Time for Janet and Kirsten. Time for their pink-tinted inter-necine struggles. Time for Michelle to assure us that – as we recall every bitter, humiliating set-to between them, every slight and sneer and episode of snark – 'the pink team have really come out on top; they've won; their relationship has got closer'. Time for Janet and Kirsten, back at the RSL, to spray on some Oro-bronze and shimmy down the catwalk next to their waddling white holograms.

'Huzzah!' Australia cries. 'Huzzah!' Kirsten's dramatic weight loss and short white dress lose some impact as she galumphs towards the camera like a puppy towards a new chew toy, but that's forgotten as soon as Janet threatens to reveal the bedroom secrets of post-chubby nooky. Neither Hayley nor Kirsten want to go there. Nobody wants to go there. But we go there anyway because a quick-thinking cameraman catches Janet's old man high-fiving his boy in the audience.

Booyah, son! Yeah I got me some a that.

Before anyone can reference Michelle and Com-mando, who are nowhere to be seen, any rising ardour is doused by a shirtless Brett. Brett fights Shannon.

Brett fights Michelle. Brett fights the Sydney Kings and breaks his arm. Brett and Mandy do the hologram shuffle, both looking good, leading to more high fives, this time from Mandy's husband, who is revealed as a personal trainer. Possibly a personal trainer with a crisis of confidence.

It'll soon be time to join everyone's favourites, Gerald and Todd, at a homecoming party, or maybe that was a leprechaun kegger, but first the Ten Network must perform the difficult manoeuvre of pivoting away from the censorious and judgmental approach to food which has characterised these last three months and diving headlong into a voluptuary celebration of the same. Having made us all feel inadequate and worthless for even thinking of fried chicken when there's so much quinoa going uneaten in the world, it's now time to wrench through the gears and make us all feel inadequate and worthless for not cooking fried chicken in goose fat with three kinds of truffle and a matched flight of wines.

Because it's *MasterChef* time again, and far from dying of embarrassment at being caught out in a shameful attempt to whip up some interest in the flagging franchise by framing it as a battle of sexes – don't all roll your eyes at once; it's dangerous – Ten decided to embrace their shame in the first ad break of the finale.

While we're still reeling from a whole new pink and blue team with which to contend, Michelle beats Shannon and the Commando to the multivitamin endorsement, before the cognitive whiplash of a KFC ad in the *Biggest Loser* grand final threatens lounge room decapitations across the country. And not just any old KFC ad, but an ad for the Colonel's fried dead birds reaching out to dudes who are so busy stuffing their faces with a week's worth of empty calories that they have to use their feet for everyday tasks such as opening doors and high-fiving other dudes while inhaling a three-piece dinner.

Then we're back to the Thunderdome and determined to end generational obesity while eating nuggets with our toes. The producers are just as determined to riff on the loser Losers who couldn't keep up with the winner Losers, and for the next 20 minutes we do some high-intensity intervals watching one unsuccessful team after another roll out with their holograms. First up are Chris and Mark, dressed in black and back together like the Blues Brothers. They emerge looking like nightclub bouncers: a little chunky, but good chunky. Powerful chunky.

Their holograms seem pretty confident too.

Holograms aren't supposed to look confident.

Anita and Cher follow them, with Anita assuring us that 'only a mother's love could save Cher'. Not her mother's cooking, but. Anita tells us she came on the show to support her daughter. Cruel people on the internet say cruel things like, 'Try harder, Anita.' From losers to winners, or potential winners, and we've thankfully left behind Hayley's uncomfortable discussion of how much further Cher's journey will be for the strangely comforting realisation that fat King Richard looks like Microsoft CEO Steve Ballmer at his panic-sweating best. Thin King Richard looks like he'd give the Lannisters a run for their money if he played a Game of Thrones with them.

There'll be a short delay however while *MasterChef* returns to extol the virtues of more goose fat, more butter, and lots more 1950 gender politics. Hungry yet? Fuggedabouddit! These KFC Twisters and gravy may only satiate your physical hunger for a few minutes, but for those few minutes your existential disgust will be also quieted. So dig in.

A fit girl chases a ninja. Not sure why. But Ninjas!

And the world's most loved cooking show is back again! Twice in one ad break, with the world's most exhausted sexist meme. Almost as though they have no dignity.

Speaking of which, it's time to recall Sam's and Jess's weigh-in when Sam, always a doughnut-half-eaten sort of guy, can take no pride in having kept his own weight below that of his ballooning offspring.

Luckily, Michelle assures us, 'This is a guy who just wants to go, and it's exciting to be around him.' Or maybe she was talking about Commando. No time to decode the subtext though, because holograms!

As Sam's carefully cultivated bouncer-look falls apart when he starts crying, Hayley reminds us that *Biggest Loser* has always had one mission: to make fat people cry and sell KFC!

Oh, wait, that's two. But surely one more little mission statement couldn't hurt? Just one wafer-thin slice? And some KFC Twisters?

Slam cut to a reaction shot, Janet back in her pink singlet and Late Elvis Period, gasping in horror, but not at all the KFC ads. Because it's time for some archival footage of Big Kev bringing the rolling thunder, providing the other Losers with a chance to go, 'The hell with self-awareness, how did that guy let himself go so badly?'

The *TBL* talent scouts outdid themselves with poor Kev, a contestant who offered the suspense and excitement of very good odds of him dying onscreen. Then it's time to revisit his epic fail in the wet T-shirt contest and we're all dying in front of our screens at home from a combination of ennui and chicken strips.

Still, Kev, eliminated early, is rockin' that basic black mafia suit, but it's Rosemary who stuns all by arriving in a Britney Spears fright mask. Hayley looks scared. Her well-scripted question about whether the trainers bullied Kev inside the camp is met with a spontaneous prepared statement that would shame the show trials of early Soviet Russia.

'I acknowledge my crimes and accept my punishment,' says Kev. 'The trainers are my comrades and work will set me free.' He shambles away across the endless steppes of the personal journey that is still ahead of him.

Journeys are big on *Biggest Loser*. Personal journeys. Journeys of discovery. Journeys of development. And journeys home, to where the heart is. And the leftovers. We follow the orange people, Robyn and Katie, our third potential winner Losers, on their journey home but get distracted by Four Times Gold Logie Winner Lisa McCune starring as Dr Lara Croft, some more KFC, natch ... oh, no, wait, those are McDonald's nuggets, for a balanced diet I guess, and at long, long last an ad for some exercise equipment nobody watching this show will ever use.

It may be the bourbon talking – yes, I've begun to drink heavily – but I find there are surprisingly few obese people in that McNugget ad.

This conundrum might bear pondering, but not now because we have no time. The moment we've all been waiting for is here. Even if you only follow *Biggest Loser* through the gossip mags. Especially if you only follow *Biggest Loser* through the gossip mags. It's time to get back to the other thing *TBL* is all about besides shouting at fat people and selling McNuggets.

The trainers! Yay! Cue the high-energy montage of lots and lots and lots of pervy shots of Michelle, Commando and Shannon getting sweaty. Cue the unseemly speculation on Twitter about Michelle's and Commando's personal lives. Then throw open the doors to the fat hologram factory and let's roll!

Will Michelle and Commando be holding hands, or like, you know, totally playing it cool? Will the producers have them next to each other, or will they place Shannon strategically between them? Would putting Shannon between them imply they needed to put Shannon between them to prevent those two perfectly hard-muscled bodies from accidentally brushing against each other and showering the first four rows of the RSL with a shower of Sexy Sparkz!?! Omigod omigod omigod why isn't this recap in *New Idea* so I could spend 3000 words on the Michelle and Commando's Sexy Sparkz imbroglio?

Because then I couldn't use words like imbroglio and we'd need baby photos.

Two pages of them. Shannon is a new dad. Huzzah for Shannon, huzzah! That's almost as exciting as the neckline of Michelle's dress. Props to wardrobe for that bad girl. And for Commando's World's

Hardest Croupier outfit. But even bigger props to the producer who fed the questions about Commando's family life into Hayley's autocue, thereby providing the Most Awkward Five Seconds of As-Live Television in Australian history.

Michelle doesn't have kids to talk about. But damn, she does have that dress, so let the cameras linger a little longer on her before the tedium of weigh-in.

Numbers numbers numbers enlivened by trying to figure out whose bingo wings look the most toned now. The usual Sunday night dragging and stretching of this segment is mercifully condensed this evening, interrupted by only one ad break, in which we learn there are no fat people in *NCIS*, unless they're plotting something; the money you save on this very generous KFC nugget deal you could put towards a massively reduced treadmill, because nobody's been buying them tonight; there are no fat people in *Fast & Furious 6* either, although Vin Diesel is looking more like a 4WD than a stripped-down street racer these days; there are no fat people with insurance from Bupa; and most surprising of all, no fat people at the *Biggest Loser* Retreat. Yes! You can have your own Chunky Gulag experience. Unless you're fat, apparently, because on the evidence before us the only people allowed in are thin, ropy Tai Chi instructors and flexible ladies in spanky pink leotards.

One last quick promo for a new Channel Ten show that implies there's a nuclear reactor about to melt down in the next suburb, and it's time for the business end of the weigh-in. Or the small business end, anyway, since we're still with the minor premiership.

Big Kev and Britney have lost a dripping wet Hayley between them, but it's not enough to dislodge Sam and Jess from the money seat. With the help of a personal trainer at home Bret and Mandy do knock them off, but only until Kirsten and Janet weigh in, *sans* the emotional baggage they left in New Zealand. Some pretty hefty baggage: it's enough to beat out the Black team and grab up the lolly. Or enough money to buy a small truckload of lollies. Not that they'll be doing that, of course. Oh no-siree-bob. Their personal journey won't ever take them past the lolly shop again. No way.

After a quick break where we learn that fat people don't chew gum but hot ladies with very white teeth do, it's time to check out Robyn and Katie's comedy act. Robyn works a little blue, especially when jumping or being pushed out of high things to her possible death, but it's getting late and we're all full of booze, fried chicken and remorse now, so WTF? It's all good fun until we flashback to the confronting black bra and granny pants moment at the start of the season.

Lingering here could get depressing, but we have the TV equivalent of high-density liquid Prozac to main-line into our eyeballs so let's get it on. Open the pod bay door and unleash the holograms! Robyn and Katie are lovin' their new bods and new frocks almost as much as their boys back home are 'lovin' their soy and linseed bread, lovin it'.

Slam cut to the boys, orders the EP.

They're not lovin' it.

Another flashback: they're coming as thick and as fast now as the free-running tears of the morbidly obese. King Richard and Princess Amber in the light blue livery of their House. The Commando is being harsh about Amber. Michelle is being harsh about Amber. King Richard is worried about the wisdom of betting the whole realm on this Amber chick. Maybe he should have got himself some more princesses. Just in case. But tonight is not the night for villainy, so now we meet good friend Richard, supportive Rich-ard, grunty, sweaty, hard-charging Richard. But not Machiavelli Richard? What happened to that guy? We loved that guy. The producers loved that guy. Online editors everywhere loved the traffic that guy could bring to their sites with just one cunning plan, or dastardly doublecross.

'Dad's been the best role model I could ever ask for,' says Amber, as she fills out the application form for the Dirty Tricks Directorate of ASIS.

A world away from Team Game of Thrones and it's time for a group hug with the people's favourite. Team Green. Gerald, the old man who worked so hard Commando had to tell him to slow down; Toddy, the good-looking boy who was bullied by the sort of bullies who watch shows like *Biggest Loser* to laugh at boys like Toddy.

Hayley has a moment. Gerald has a moment. Little Sophie, who this was all about, has a moment.

Meanwhile in the wings, King Richard sharpens his dagger.

Another moment from Hayley! If Hayley Moments conferred a kilogram weigh-in advantage we could all go home now before Gerald and Toddy wasted away before our eyes.

But we can't, because it's time for the last weigh-in, and a reminder that someone is going to take home $200 000 minus tax. Although, really, nobody reminds anybody about their tax liability.

One last check-in with the trainers. Commando is looking like he'd rather be somewhere else. Michelle has crossed her legs towards Commando. Does that mean something? It must mean something, if only a couple of pages of speculation in the gossip rags next week.

King Richard gives Toddy a rub on the head,

breaking character, but Toddy is just so adorbs even this Shakespearean villain can't help himself.

It's not enough to redeem him in the eyes of the chicken-eating peasantry, however, and a cheer goes up across the land as the Green team wins out on the scales. The King Is Dead. The King Is Dead.

Wait. The King is giving Toddy another head rub. Like a regular guy? He's breaking character again. And formerly fat people are smiling at him! And each other! Is it possible that King Richard was not who we were led to believe? Is it possible this whole show has lied to us?

I don't know and there's no time because Katie and Robyn are stepping up and weighing and needing to lose one whole Commando to deny little Sophie the prize money for her medical treatment, and they've done it and they've done it and they've done it, and the audience erupts and the glitter foil spills from heaven and Hayley promises something about coming back to do something to the fattest town in Australia and as we fade away we spy Shannon one last time, but no Commando and no Michelle.

And no Tiffany.

But she was a ninja and could have been there the whole series and we would never have known.

Sydney Morning Herald, June 2013

Yoga for the modern bro

You are receiving this email because you are a bro who needs yoga in his life. Or you know a bro who needs yoga in his life. And all bros do, so that is why you received this email.

Before you stab viciously at the delete button, examine your feelings right now. That sick sense of dizziness which came out of nowhere when you opened this email? That sudden free-floating rage? That pain in your arm and crushing weight on your chest? That's the absence of yoga silently screaming at full volume in your chakra.

Yoga is not just for thin white women in Lululemon any more. It's for the men who never realised how uncomfortably close they could get to those thin white women in Lululemon, while sweating and grunting in a way that would see them arrested outside the nonjudgmental safe space of our fully equipped yoga studio, or as we prefer to call it, Xtreme Namastud Flexing Factory. Booyah!

The *Washington Post* reported just last week that

desperate yoga instructors have increasingly been trying to make their classes stand out from thousands of competing yoga instructors with yoga and beer, or yoga and marijuana, or even yoga and goats. *WaPo* asks, 'Have we reached peak namaste?'

Here at the Xtreme Namastud Flexing Factory we say NO!

Not until you've experienced yoga *and* beer *and* marijuana *and* goats all in one comparatively affordable package.

All modern bros whose PayPal, Square Cash or credit card payments clear after enrolment in my Yoga for the Mo' Bro workshop will learn to replace their feelings of howling emptiness and inner pain with a simple direct debit of $49.99 (goats not included) for every month they wish to unburden themselves of karmic and bodily suffering and that one low-low payment.

Don't delete.

And don't unsubscribe!

Our webmasters have made that process so punishingly user-hostile that you will need the premium-level subscription to Yoga for the Mo' Bro ($69.99/ month, goats included) to recover, after failing to even loosen the tangled knot of densely impacted rage you are guaranteed to experience while failing to unsubscribe.

You could choose not to click or tap on the 'Buy Now' link below, or on the dozens of invisible links to the same high-pressure sales page embedded in the text of this email (although, like unsubscribing, we've made that virtually fucking impossible too), but you would be choosing to fail. You would be giving in to fear. Fear that you are not good enough. Fear that you don't measure up.

Because you don't.

As super-enlightened yoga bros, our yogi masters are more self-satisfied and condescending than any other similarly priced instructors, and without their overbearing magic ass-pants attitude and thinly veiled contempt, you cannot hope to achieve even half a backwards tortoise downward doggy-style with any of the thin white girls or almond MILFs who make up three-quarters of the 37 million yoga-doing population of America, according to *WaPo*.

If you think you don't need yoga in your life and we don't need your account details in our database, just ask yourself what happens when your last beer rolls under the couch, or the TV remote is infuriatingly stranded just out of reach over your shoulder.

Are you going to get up and reach for them? Like some sort of animal?

Or will you impress all the bendy girls and make your inflexible male rivals seethe with envy when you retrieve both adult beverage and magic channel wand like a limbersexual sofa captain?

You want that.

She'll want you.

And we'll take your credit card details now, captain.

aliensideboob.com, March 2017

Leisure Suit Larry and the joystick of destiny

He respawned. And died inside.

He died a little more inside every time he came back. A couple of pixels winking out, his renders growing furred and jaggier. Not so you'd notice any difference from one life to the next. Unless you were Larry.

Larry noticed. Larry felt the creeping murmur in his head, the pouring dark at the edge of his vision. He was degrading. Being scrubbed, deleted subroutine by subroutine. And it was accelerating.

He respawned and checked himself over. Ninety-four bucks. Always 94. Cheap fucking code monkeys wouldn't even slip him a Benjamin. A lousy fucking C-note, what was it to them? A couple of lines of code, maybe?

But no. There were always 94 simoleons in his pocket. That subroutine never degraded. He never came back and found himself with half a rock or a lazy grand.

Ninety-four dollars, a cheap necklace, not even gold-plated – he'd been embarrassed to find that out down at the pawn shop, lemme tell ya – and his 'leisure suit' of course. A yellowing, ur-Travolta monstrosity as specced up by some dev who'd never set foot in a disco because he was more comfortable scaling the boobs on a Lara Croft wannabe from merely bodacious to impossibly humungous than he was dealing with a real woman.

He grunted at the feeling of his insides being turned inside out like an old sock.

Best he didn't think about the ladies. The code monkeys hadn't done him any favours there. Best just stay the hell away from any decision tree involving women.

A trail of tears, my friend. A trail of fucking tears.

Larry took a moment to turn full circle, orienting himself.

An alleyway. Dumpsters overflowing with discarded junk-food artefacts. Boxes. Always with the boxes, because destructible environments were always more immersive.

But then this environment was entirely destructible, wasn't it? Everything in the world of atoms could be atomised, violently, or simply allowed to succumb to the ravages of entropy. Although, in Larry's case, the former tended to trump the latter every fucking time.

He could smell the decay of the real city. The old sweat and urine of the hobo passed out against the wall a little further down the alley. Fried food. Bad meat. Petrochemicals and dogshit.

You never saw any damn dogs in this place, but their crap was everywhere. He wondered sometimes if feral packs came in from the desert to scavenge, leaving their scat behind.

He should have got moving, but he stood, unable to move because there seemed no good reason for him to move. He knew how this would end. The way it always ended. Kinetically. Ballistically. Bloodily.

Game Over.

What was the point? Seriously. What was the fucking point of it? He could just stand here and wait out the process. Declare for entropy this time. Wait for the years to overtake him … and if that didn't work? Wait for the quantum bonds that held him together, the mere chance that stopped his personal universe from disassembling itself, his coded arrangement of bits-turned-to-atoms simply phase shifting from coherent to its opposite. A trillion trillion tiny aspects of Larry suddenly dispersed throughout creation. Chances were, sometime before the heat death of this wider universe, it would happen. After all, was it any less likely than what had already happened?

He sighed and stepped off, walking towards the light. No revelation space beckoned him. It was just a four-lane strip somewhere well shy of downtown Lost Wages.

Yeah, he knew that wasn't the name of this dump, but it had always been Lost Wages to him. Not just because he was coded that way, but because he had to have something to hold on to. Some reason to believe he could get back. Otherwise where was he?

In hell.

Like Bill Murray.

Yeah, he'd watched that movie once. What? You think all Larry does is pay hookers and play the slots? Maybe once, but that was a long time ago in a galaxy far, far away. Yeah, seen all them too. And he'll tell you, if you can put aside your prejudice, that George Lucas was misunderstood in the end.

But Bill Murray. *Groundhog Day*? Yeah, he was in hell. Some bullshit Buddhist version of hell, maybe, where he reincarnated over and over until he got it right, but Larry knew that was bullshit because there was no getting it right. He'd tried. Genuinely tried. Taken piano lessons and everything. But Murray was using cheat codes. Murray played on the easy setting.

Larry got dumped into hardcore mode.

No replays. No walk thrus. No practice levels.

First couple of days he'd spent in the real, he soiled his leisure suit in terror. First couple of weeks, he near died of exposure and starvation.

First time he had actually died? Stabbed in the groin by a midget he'd tried to mug for three bucks. He'd heard tell of a taco van four or five blocks south of Balzar. Six tacos for $2.99. Totally worth getting stabbed in the dick for.

And the first time he respawned? Less terror, but closer to madness, when he realised he was in hell.

Larry dragged himself towards that brightly lit thoroughfare. Back towards hell. First cars he'd seen here were long, big-ass American chariots. White-walled tyres and even fake wood panelling. The street traffic ahead of him was still thick with old clunkers, but it also hummed with sleek hybrids and small jelly-bean shaped vehicles with roofs and bonnets covered in solar cells.

Time moved on here. Everything moved on. Except Larry.

Ninety-four dollars.

His hand crept into his pants pocket by habit, finding the crumpled, greasy bills where they always lay. Four twenties, a ten-spot and change. Not nearly enough. Not for where he needed to be.

There'd always been rumours.

Whispers among the non-player characters. Things unspoken between the narrative leads.

The 'disappeared'.

He'd even known a few. Fawn. Faith. Eve. All of

them gone. And now he knew where.

Of course everyone talked about the traffic that came back the other way. Those idiots, usually kids, got themselves pulled into a game. That *Tron* douchebag. Those *eXistenZ* assholes. Emilio fucking Estevez. Oh man, how they'd all laughed at that one back in the old hot tub.

But nobody ever talked openly about the two-way trade. About what had happened to Fawn and Faith and Eve. And now, of course, what had happened to him.

He took the folded bills from his pocket. They weren't crisp or clean. The edge of the banknotes felt almost frayed. Like him.

Ninety-four dollars. He could get a bus to the west coast for that, but he wouldn't even make it halfway east. No riding the pooch to deliverance for Larry. It was always the way. Years he'd spent researching, planning his escape. Although most of his 'research' had been restricted to the public library. First in the stacks and then later on the net. He sought out stories. He found out things. He knew there had to be a way.

If those kids went in and he went out, there had to be a conduit, a passage. And call him a poorly realised two-dimensional character, but he thought that a good place to look for it might be one of the consoles he knew to be open to traffic. If he could just find one.

Get to it. It might be as simple as laying his hands on the joystick or the controller. It might be enough to transport him to another world.

But it was always so hard to get an even break in this place. Not just the city, the whole country. You started off with 90 bucks and change in your pocket here, you were likely to die with that amount or significantly less credited to your name. There were so few ways to escape the trap. He'd tried them all. Working, hustling, stealing, rolling midgets. They all crapped out in the end. When you started poor in this game there was no levelling up.

Still, what choice did he have? Bill Murray could throw himself in front of a train again and again, but eventually he'd find his moment of satori.

Larry had tried that. Failed. Now he had to try it his way.

He stepped out onto the main street.

And died.

'Har! Har! Har! Looks like clean-up on aisle four.'

The Duke stowed away his chain gun and ducked down below the roofline. He'd had to make like a cheap hooker and blow quickly. The cops on this level were murder. Worse than pigmen.

He relit his stogie, which had gone out while he waited on his target to appear. Stogies did that here. They went out and cops shot at you for wasting a dude and everything was confusing and ugly and he was in hell. Duke Nukem had been in hell for years.

But he had a plan, damn it. He was gonna get his damned level bonus and get the fuck outta here. Level up and level out.

He knew how now. Knew not to spray down the NPC like mutant pigmen. Knew to pick his targets. Like Larry.

Nobody ever missed Larry. He was a human decoy.

But damn if he didn't spawn at some random fucking points on the map. He could take forever to track down.

But the Duke had forever.

Smith Journal, March 2014

Knocked off your perch

The bar was crowded. Too crowded. Two weeks before Christmas on a hot Sunday afternoon. It was a new place, another addition to the city's rapidly growing number of craft-beer venues. The tiny kitchen turned out beer-friendly snacks like deep-fried cheese. A corner verandah provided a shady spot under the thick green foliage of some old-growth trees. It was all just a little bit too perfect.

We arrived three-quarters of an hour before the agreed drinking time. Long enough to lay down a solid base of deep-fried cheese. We were but two in number then, but like Mary and Joseph kicking about Bethlehem looking for a half-decent craft-beer outlet, preferably in a renovated manger with the original fit-out playfully adapted to reuse in a hospitality setting, we found no room at the inn. No fried cheese for us.

What to do? In the heaving flux of the crowd, occasional gaps opened up. A bar stool here, a table there. But there was neither rhyme nor reason to the process. No pattern to be discerned. A couple of wheyfaced hipsters, who ambled in five minutes after me, walked right up to a table, vacated just as they arrived, and took it as though they had been waiting far too long for a pale ale and a plate of fried cheese cubes. Which they hadn't. Because they were stupid table-jumping hipsters. This seemed to happen again and again as we orbited the bar, increasingly desperate. I can drink on the move, and I did in this case. You have to keep up your fluids after all. But this is not the way of a civilised man, forever jostling and being jostled on the endless search for a place he might set up and spend a few hours sampling the beer menu.

After a while, we went with my preferred option. To perch.

When perching, your site selection is paramount. Choose the wrong perch and you will spend the day being elbow-jogged while stupid hipsters wander aim-lessly in off the street and take the table that should rightly have been yours. Choose the wrong perch and you will never know the joy of fried cheese.

I judged the best perch in this situation to be at the corner, where the outside deck wrapped around the block under the shade of the old elms. From this vantage point I could surveil both arms of the deck and cast my scan over the interior of the bar. I could lean against the fence, as though I had chosen to do just that, because I am a handsome leaning dude who damn well chose to stand in that very spot and not some wretched endlessly shuffling refugee with nowhere to drink, or even to stand, and not a single cube of fried Australian cheese to his credit.

The minutes ticked by. The quarter hours. A half hour. And still I perched.

I came to recognise the natural enemy of the percher, the shuffling horde of rootless shamblers who were not content to put down roots and invest the time and effort necessary to make this bar their own. Damn their eyes. They could have been at any bar. Why did they have to come here?

I thought my perching was about to pay off when the table next to which I had perched began to make moves as if to leave. I switched my stance, subtly turning one shoulder towards them, signalling to the loud Americans perched next to me that they should not imagine that just because they were loud and American they'd be rolling in over my claim on that table.

The Americans backed off. Victory was mine. But then … *la catastrophia*!

The leaving party decided to stay for 'just one more'. And some fried cheese!

Oh noes, they would be here for hours. Even worse: their initial move to depart had drawn the attention of every rat-bastard shambler in the bar. They rolled on us like thunderheads out of the western sky.

Back, you filthy bastards, get back, I roared. In my head. They backed off only when they too could see the lying hounds who had misled us so cruelly had no intentions of giving up their cushy little spot. In fact, I suspect they only pretended to do so to taunt and mock us for their sport.

Not only did they stay for 'just one more'; they were still encamped there when I left three hours later. Having secured the table next to them. By the disciplined application of the ancient and noble art of lurking. Not shambling.

brisbanetimes.com.au, December 2014

There is a level 200 squirtle at the end of this think piece

It is a truth universally acknowledged that a fad in possession of a following must be in want of a think piece, and there is no fad bigger this week than Pokémon Go. Having opened our think piece with an overused classical reference for the old people who were paying attention, it is time to move on to the lucrative clickbait which drew the much more valuable young people here like a Pokémon Go addict to a secluded car park in search of the rare cartoon thingies.

Note the elegant segue into our hot take about the Pokémon Go thingies. It was very well done. But not as well done as this second paragraph with which we can now scare you because with so many people talking about the Pokémon Goes right now, the Pokémons are being used by violence gangs to lure people who are just like our readers into traps. Analytics tells us there is an 83 per cent chance you are just like our readers so it could be you trapped by a violence gang who used a Pokémon to trap you. In a secluded car park. Scary.

Nonetheless, no scary think piece about this current Pokémon craze is worth the pixels it's written on without data, because calling the same old thing data journalism is way more sexy than calling it plain old journalism, which isn't hot or sexy, and the Pokémon kids today are all about the modern sexy things. Does this mean our kids could be using their phones to have Pokémon sex with each other? Any legitimate think piece must say yes.

Brisbane Times girl reporter and verified young person Ms Amy Remeikis agrees, having been inconvenienced to the point of tweeting about it by an unknowable number of Pokémon Go addicts pointing their sex phones at things and getting in her way in the mall yesterday.

'People have lost their minds,' she wrote. 'They are standing around the mall pointing their phones at things and yelling.'

Some of the things they were pointing their sex phones at and yelling about may even have been a dead body, because that actually happened and was widely reported.

'I just got up and went for my little walk, a walk to catch Pokémon,' said 19-year-old Shayla Wiggens, a young girl who found a dead body while looking for Pokémon. Initial reports did not initially indicate Shayla found the body in the Queen Street Mall but it makes you think, doesn't it? That's what think pieces do.

Increasingly, we live in a world where commentators are forced into ever more ridiculous comments by the need to posture on the latest thing. But this Pokémon Go phenomenon is the most serious issue I have ever commented on late yesterday afternoon as deadline loomed.

Finally, here in the last par, it would be appropriate to make a knowing reference to Pikachu, but I don't actually know what that is.

brisbanetimes.com.au, July 2016

DOMESTIC AFFAIRS

He died with a felafel in his hand

He died with a felafel in his hand. We found him on a beanbag with his chin resting on the top button of a favourite flannelette shirt. He'd worn the shirt when we interviewed him for the empty room a week or so before. We were having one of those bad runs, where you seem to interview about 30 people every day and they are all total munters. We really took this guy in desperation. He wasn't A-list, didn't have a microwave or anything like that, and now both he and the felafel roll were cold. Our first dead housemate. At least we'd got some bond off him.

We had no idea he was a junkie, otherwise he never would've got that room. You let one junkie in the house and you may as well let them all in. We had another secret junkie live with us once. Melissa. She was okay, but her boyfriend stole all of my CDs. Told me some Japanese guy, a photographer, took them and if I went to this club on Wednesday nights I could probably find him there. Yeah right.

Melissa, on the other hand, ran a credit scam out

of the same house. Months after she left, a couple of debt collectors came around looking for Rowan Corcoran. It was the identity she'd set up, but we didn't know that. We were very helpful, because bills had been turning up for this Corcoran prick for months. We didn't know who he was, just some mystery guy racking up thousands of dollars in debt and sending the bills to our place. We sat the debt collectors down in the living room with a cup of tea. Showed them all the other bills that had been arriving for Mr Corcoran. When they saw that the last bill was for Qantas tickets to America their shoulders sort of slumped. I've still got those bills. $35 000 worth.

But Melissa was okay. In fact she was a real babe. She used to steal food for the house from this restaurant she worked in. (If you're reading this, Melissa, we really appreciated the food.) There were five of us living at Kippax Street at that stage. Everyone was on the dole or Austudy or minimum wage. The house was typical Darlinghurst, this huge, dark, damp terrace with yellowed ceilings, green carpet with cigarette burns and brown, torn-up furniture. We'd sit around on Tuesday night waiting for Melissa to get home with our stolen dinner. She usually walked through the door just before *Twin Peaks* came on, so there was this nice warm feeling in the house as we all sat in front of the teev scarfing down the free stuff. On a good night, when someone's cheque had come through, we had a couple of beers to share round. And on a great night, when someone, usually Melissa, had scored, we'd pull out the bucket bong and get completely whacked. On those nights, that nice warm feeling was really close. It wrapped you up like your dad's old jumper, kept you safe. On those nights, you could delude yourself that share housing, which is all about deprivation and economic necessity, was really about something else: a friendly sort of half-sensible descendant of the communal ideal. But it never lasts. Never holds together. Somebody always moves on, or loses their mind, or dies with a felafel in his hand and you're on the road again.

Jeffrey!

That was the dead guy's name. It got away from me for a minute there, but I knew it started with a 'J'. He died watching *Rage* with the sound turned down. One of the hip young inner-city cops who turned up to investigate said he probably snuffed it halfway through the hot 100. Just like a junkie. There was a nightclub stamp on his wrist, bruises up and down his arm. The felafel's chilli and yoghurt sauce had leaked from the roll and run down his hand in little white rivulets. For a brief, perverse moment it seemed to me that he himself had sprung a leak, a delicate stream of liquid heroin escaping from the seams of his fingers.

I've seen a hundred lives pass through the bleary, kind of sleep-deprived landscape of a dozen different share houses, but Jeffrey's was the only one that ever fetched up and died on a beanbag. The others all moved along their own weird trajectories. They were never still. Everyone was constantly mobile or wanting to be – moving targets, random drifters and people whose lives rested on nothing more stable than inertia. Dead souls every one. Some of them now work for gigantic weapons corporations or drug cartels. They've got these incredible lives. Jet travel. Credit cards. Respect, even fear, from those top-hatted guys who stand in front of the Hyatt. But if they were housemates of mine, I've seen them bludging meals from the Krishnas. Or sitting on the lounge room floor in home-brand underwear with all the windows blacked out and hundreds of candles pushing back the dark. Not doing much. Just sitting there. Or smashing 500 empty beer bottles into a million jagged pieces on the kitchen floor while grey-ing burger patties slowly peel away from the ceiling … Slowly, slowly, slowly … then plop – impaled on the waiting fangs of glass below. Or sitting in front of the television for two days straight, with giant frilled lizards clinging to their shoulders, a bowl of magic mushrooms by their feet, their weeping bloodshot eyes the shape of little rectangles.

Madness, as one flatmate of mine used to say with just a hint of satisfaction in his voice. Things get out of control all the time in share houses. It's not just a matter of the rent slipping behind, or the washing piling up. People flip over the line. Way over. I know about this. Been there myself a couple of times. One place, Duke Street – home of the smashed stubbies and falling burger patties – was nothing but a madhouse. A huge rambling kind of place, an ex-brothel, we all thought, because there were so many rooms in there. Bedrooms where bedrooms shouldn't ought to be and so on. We were paying $11 a week each between the ten or eleven of us living there. We were never completely sure of the number because of the continual drop-ins and disappearances and the strange case of Satomi Tiger.

I know you're just thinking – what the hell is a Satomi Tiger? Well, we're sitting on the lino floor of the living room one night – actually we had two living rooms in this weird house, but we turned the other one into a basketball court – and we're watching TV, as usual. And this Japanese girl walks in wearing these audacious tiger-striped pants and a poo-brown imitation dead fur thing. 'Good eve-en-ing,' she says. 'I move in now.' And that was all. She had no other English. She drops a wad of cash on the TV and wanders off to find a room. We're all just sitting there thinking, What the hell is this? But then again, she's dropped this wad on the teev so who cares?

We found out later that Satomi Tiger had met our invisible flatmate Tim on his last trip to Asia. The one which ended up with him being investigated for espionage and committed to an insane asylum in Hong Kong. You can see Tim in the miniseries *Bangkok Hilton*. He plays three different bit parts, most notably that of a drunken buffoon in a boat. A frighteningly accurate performance. Tim escaped from the asylum with the help of a dead friend, also called Tim, but he was always a little elsewhere after that. He'd met Satomi Tiger in Japan and invited her to visit him in Queensland. She took him up on the offer. The only thing was, we never really knew where Tim was at any given moment. When Satomi Tiger arrived, rumour had him cutting sugar cane in the north. Whatever. It didn't bother her, and it didn't really bother us. It was that kind of house. The set-up with the rent, for instance, was very suspicious. We'd send a cash cheque every two or three weeks to this post office box in the western suburbs, deep in serial killer territory. We never got any receipts but we never got any hassles either. There was a phone number to call in emergencies, which we used when the bathroom looked like it was going to fall off the end of the house one time, but there was this spooky message at the other end.

'There's no one here,' *click*, *brrrrr* ...

At that stage, I'd quit my job in Canberra and was kicking around Brisbane, wasting my life again. Duke Street seemed the perfect place for it. The floating population, the lack of furniture, the crazy tilting floors, the freight train line which ran through the backyard, the hallucinogenic mushrooms in the front yard, the tree which grew through the bedroom window, the constant low-grade harassment by the Department of Social Security, the week-long drinking binges, the horror, the horror.

Early in my stay there, I took a four-week job as a typist with the Department of Primary Industries. They had these reports that were seven years overdue. I'm not joking. They stressed this point to me. Seven years. Probably dog years too. So I'm bashing away on a word processor, getting into the Zen of typing because it's so dull if I actually stop to think what I'm doing, my head will implode and I'll be this sultana-headed guy walking around town. Anyway, after a while I look around the typing pool and I get this huge Fear. The Fear grabs me by the heart and squeezes like a bastard for three days straight. It's saying This Is Your Life. So I enrol in Law at Queensland University.

God, I hated it. A few weeks into semester the first assignment is due. I've missed a few classes and my notes aren't that great. I'm surrounded by these carnivorous teenagers, fresh-smelling, label-wearing, beady-eyed little rat bastards who never lend me their notes. On the day I've set aside to do this assignment, I can't find anything, not even the question sheet, and I flip over the line. I start screaming. It sounds like something from the jungle or a subterranean prison for the criminally insane where all the inmates have devolved into these lower forms. They don't even look human any more and they're taking messages straight from the brain stem, primitive reptilian urgings. I've got this working through me. I kick a hole in the wall and pick up a golf club and charge into the living room and start laying about me letting go with more of the monster screeches. Well the other guys in the house, they've been there. They sort of hang back and watch the show. Get a beer from the fridge, that sort of thing. And eventually I do calm down. I'm not that fit, and my arms go tired and I deflate like an old balloon. I realise everyone is watching me, grinning hugely. I shrug. Means nothing. An hour later we found Satomi Tiger hiding in a cupboard. She'd never stay in the same room as me after that.

Madness, you see. Things getting out of control. It's one of the constants of share housing. Now I'll allow that most of the time it doesn't get to the stage of kicking out walls and terrifying obscure tiger-suited Japanese girls, but it's always there, a sort of chaotic potential snaking about under the surface of things, rearing its head only briefly in the course of arguments over phone bills or cleaning up.

Like, I used to share a flat with a bank clerk called Derek. Derek the bank clerk pitched a tent, literally, on the living room floor. The house budget needed one more rent payer but had no more rooms, and Derek the bank clerk needed a place to stay but was kind of a tight-arse about money. So he puts up this tent in the corner of the living room and pays half-rent. Crawls into this thing at night. Falls out of it in the morning. A real fringe-dwelling bank clerk. It worked for a while. But Derek was very territorial. Used to gradually creep that tent across the floor into the television-watching area. Liked to poke his head out of the flaps and watch the ABC. During the day, when he was gone, I'd push it back. At night, he'd creep it out again. It started small at first, a few inches one way, a few inches back. But the confrontation went on. He jumped his border out a whole foot. I pushed back a metre. He'd take two metres. I'd break a tent pole. And the whole time, never a word was spoken. It was a lucky thing we didn't keep guns in the house. You could feel it moving towards a Red Wedding season finale, but fortunately the bank transferred him and this taxi driver moved in. We said, 'No tents, taxi driver, just throw a mattress here on the floor.' That was cool with him. He liked being in the centre of things. But it raised another problem: made it difficult to keep the flat tidy.

I have to jump a couple of houses here and tell you about the worst place I ever lived, absolutely the dirtiest filthiest place, King Street. A rat died in the living room at King Street and we didn't know. There was at least six inches of compacted crap between our feet and the floor, and old ratty, he must've crawled in there and died of pleasure. A visitor uncovered him while groping about for a beer. I don't want to go into detail on King Street yet but remind me later to tell you about the open door policy in the toilet, and the pubic hair competition and how the kitchen got so bad we had to do all of our cooking in the backyard.

You shouldn't get the idea that all share houses are like that though. I've lived in some beautiful places. Really I have. Mostly they stayed that way because women lived there too – not always, but mostly. I don't want to be sexist about this, but there's something about men living with men that unleashes the beast.

Gay guys are okay to live with on that score. They're hyper-clean. Problem is, they're also a bit sensitive about the gay thing. Or they want you to be a bit sensitive about the gay thing. I had a housemate come out to me once. This guy, Dirk, appeared in the living room at one or two in the morning when I was putting the moves on Nina, this girl who also lived there. There were tear tracks on his face as he stood there staring at us. I was giving Nina this foot massage at the time. I mean, really giving her the works, so I didn't notice him at first. But he starts snuffling and kind of whimpering and we spin around. I've got this girl's foot in my crotch and there stood Dirk, sort of staring and snuffling and of course I think, oh noes, Dirk's got a thing for Nina. The moment's destroyed as you can imagine, and then Dirk says, 'I'm gay.'

Whew! What a relief.

Now I can see old Dirk is doing it tough. And I like to think myself a broad-minded sort of guy. So I say to him, 'That's cool. We always thought you were.' This is what I have instead of male sensitivity. Anyway, Nina sits through the horrors of the night with him and I had to go to bed dreaming of her soft, milky white feet wrapped around my dick. So I ask you, who got the raw end of that deal? Funny thing is, Nina and Dirk hated each other. They were always having these knockdown drag-out jihads about stuff like whether the tuna chunks went in the cupboard or the fridge.

Nina moved out shortly after that, so this other girl Emma and I got to live with Dirk while he was coming to terms with his sexuality. The trouble wasn't with him being gay (we did pass a house by-law that banned kissing and fondling on the lounge room couch, but it applied to all sexual orientations). The trouble was that we didn't care he was gay. So we'd say these brutal things which he'd pick up on his sophisticated gay radar. We'd say, 'How about cleaning the shower, Dirk?' and he'd decode it as, 'You filthy little arse-bandits should all be nailed to a tree.'

Do you think we could get old Dirk to clean the bathroom? No way. He wasn't buying into any hetero-fascist sterility conspiracy. 'Gay men are dying!' he'd screech at a bemopped Emma on cleaning day. He eventually inherited half a million bucks and moved out to set up a gay men's retreat in northern Queensland. Hope his gay brothers put him straight about cleaning things.

Don't know how Dirk would have coped with finding Jeffrey the junkie all cold and blue spilled over the beanbag. An actual dead guy as opposed to the rhetorical gay ones which littered his post-closet conversation. Seeing as Dirk never surfaced before lunchtime, I guess it would've been academic even if he and Jeffrey had lived under the same roof. One thing is for sure. He wouldn't have cleaned up the mess, so he wouldn't have found the thousand bucks Jeffrey had stashed away in his room. The cops told us to stay out of there until the science guys had come around to check it out properly for crimes and shit but we snuck in about ten minutes after they left. It didn't take long to find the cash rolled up and hidden away in the battery compartment of his ghetto blaster and since he'd lied to us about being a junkie and brought a world of hurt down on our home, we figured it was only fair that Jeffrey make this posthumous contribution to the kitty.

Duffy and Snellgrove, September 1994

The magpie war

Heed me now, magpie, you do not want this war. Ask your allies the possums and those vile, warted invaders the cane toads what it means when JB brings war upon you. Oh? What's that? You can't find them to ask? That is because I have driven them from my lands, just as you too will be driven into far exile if you dare transgress again.

You know of what I speak, magpie. You have your realm and I have mine, and the freshly baked, hot buttered muffin which I was enjoying for breakfast yesterday morning lay well within the boundaries of my realm, not yours. The clean and folded laundry over which you released quite frankly startling amounts of stinking guano as you made off with my muffin lay well within my realm, within my TV room in fact, which is about as realmy as it gets, you squawking thief.

Were this the only incursion I have suffered we might yet put our differences aside and live in peace, but the muffin was far from an isolated incident, was it not? And that was not the first time my laundry has been used as a convenient aiming point for your apparently limitless streams of hot bottom juice. Likewise, do not imagine I am unaware of your daring raids on the cat's food bowl. Rest assured I have not forgotten the time you made off with my chicken sandwich, leaving yet another mocking squirt of avian arse *jus* in exchange. These are not the isolated incidents that might be expected when two great powers rub up hard against each other. This is a clear and present and ongoing violation of the borders which rightly separate us.

This is why I came upon you in the full regalia of battle, a large cushion imprinted with the image of a fearsome war terrier as my shield, a hot-pink feather duster my sword, it being the only sword within reach when you attacked. Am I to take it from your shrieking protestations that you object to the legitimate defence of my realm and my muffin? Well prepare yourself for disappointment, magpie. For as long as you see fit to cross from the outside world to the inside, you will find me arrayed for battle, my terrible, swift pink sword poised to strike, the sturdy puppy pillow shield raised firm in anticipation of your counterattack, just as soon as I've washed the bird poop off it after last time. I did not ask for this war, magpie, but as you have asked for it, you shall have it. And though you may have started hostilities between us on your own terms, I will most assuredly finish them on mine.

brisbanetimes.com.au, September 2015

I have frozen my last toad

I must remember to take that cane toad out of the freezer before the kids go looking for iceblocks later. Although, maybe I should get some new iceblocks too. I just checked on my chilled-out little friend, and he appears to have broken out of the double-layered plastic shopping bags in which he was supposed to sleep the big sleep.

How is it we are reduced to this?

The cane toad crossed me. Crawled into my BBQ cover and set up home. In a civilised society – that is, a society in which the needs of the apex predator, me, are catered to above those of an interloping toad – there'd be no question of JB having to chase a lumpy, jumping little turd of feral nastiness around the garden with a couple of plastic shopping bags. JB would just say to his young lad, 'Boy, go get Daddy's shotgun. Or five iron. I need to work on my swing.'

But noooooo. We don't do that sort of thing any more. A civilised man would never even consider discharging a barrel or two of 12-gauge pest control in a built-up area. A civilised man would never tee off on

Bufo marinus because the neighbours might complain. No. Not about the unavoidable consequence of toad bits describing unpredictable ballistic arcs into their stupid bird baths or geranium beds. No. About the cruelty! The cruelty, I tell you.

Enough is enough.

I have frozen my last toad.

My freezer is meant for speed-chilling beer slushies, not gentling warty vermin into their long good night. Besides the indignity of crabbing around after said toad yesterday, I now have to throw away a perfectly good packet of Zooper Doopers which I'm pretty sure the randy little shit attempted to fuck in a last desperate attempt to pass on its DNA.

And then, of course, I'll probably have to defrost.

I wasn't due to defrost for another two or three years. The advancing ice cave walls had not yet filled up the entirety of my freezer space. There was still room for a packet of Zooper Doopers and one horny toad.

I don't like to blame Campbell Newman for everything – that's what Tony Abbott is for – but I blame him for this.

Mr Premier, go get me my shotgun and the right to discharge it against Mister Marinus in defence of my BBQ cover. Or it's over between us.

brisbanetimes.com.au, January 2014

Problem solver needed.
Moral flexibility a must

Let's say a guy had a possum problem. Hypothetically speaking, you understand. And let's say that our guy was in the market for another guy to take care of his possum problem. How would our guy go about securing the services of this other guy who would have, let's say, just hypothetically, a certain *moral flexibility* on and around the question of dealing with said possum?

Understand that our guy with the possum problem, he's a good guy. And this possum which is proving to be such a problem, this thing is the Adolf Hitler of possums. Our guy, he's put up with a lotta shit. Literally. Our guy is not the sort to complain about having to mop up hundreds of little poop bullets getting sprayed at him, machine gun–style, from the rafters under his house every day. Our guy is not the sort of guy who goes a bit wobbly just because he has to clean up thick black pools of toxic possum arse leakage just to get to his damned office every day. Our guy is a lovely fellow and not at all stuck up.

But our guy has his limits. And being mocked every day for months by an evil plush toy, that's well beyond the limit of what a reasonable guy should be expected to endure. Our guy's place smells like a zoo, goddamn it. Or it would, you know, if this weren't simply a hypothetical situation we were discussing here. A hypothetical, let's say, in which this possum has taken to shitting in the washing machine, spraying its liquid arse spray all over the beer fridge, and laughing at our guy as he shakes his fist at the possum in debilitating and impotent rage.

Our guy has had enough!

Enough, I tell you!

Hypothetically speaking, you understand.

And while we are speaking, just hypothetically, our guy would really like to know if anybody knows of another guy, one in the problem-solving business, who might be amenable to solving the problem of this possum *permanently*. Our guy is not interested in folk remedies like leaving snake droppings around the place. Do you know how difficult it is to secure snake faeces retail?

Nor is our guy interested in just setting a trap full of delicious tropical fruit for our fat little friend to relax in while waiting for a licensed and ethical possum trapper to carry him ever so gently up the street for nine or maybe even ten metres, there to gently release him into the nearest tree, as required by law, where Adolf might enjoy a nap while brewing up a vintage batch of toxic bottom spray and arse bullets.

The possum guy who our guy would be after, in a purely hypothetical sense, would be the sort of guy who lights cigarillos off the rundown heels of leather biker boots made from baby harp seals. He would probably have some interesting facial scars, perhaps a twitch, and as I said, not just a willingness but a degenerate enthusiasm for looking the other way when certain inconvenient animal protection laws were violated, possibly with explosives.

This is the sort of guy our guy would probably want to speak to. Hypothetically.

A guy like that, he could probably name his own price for solving a problem like this. Permanently.

And, you know, hypothetically.

brisbanetimes.com.au, April 2015

Dog beach

I took the dog down to the beach, as is my wont. Once or twice a year we sojourn to Byron Bay. There's a Mexican joint there, at the top of the main street, which does excellent margaritas. This alone is reason enough to visit, but the main purpose of driving for a couple of hours is to walk the dog.

The local government authorities maintain a relaxed attitude on the question of hounds set loose upon their sands. Most beachside local government authorities are implacably opposed to allowing dogs anywhere near the beach, but Byron, being held in the thrall of Greens and vegans and winged fairies, has set aside an entire bay upon which you can walk your best friend.

Sophie, my ageing labrador, loves it, of course. A city dog, she is walked at least once a day, occasionally even two or three times. But I can understand the regular round of pissed-upon telephone poles, car tyres and dead possums grows stale with repetition. The legacy of her breeding calls. Labradors descend from a line of sturdy water-fowling hounds and are seldom happier than when they are wet. Being wet and chewing experimentally on a captured bird is, for them, the first step on the happy path to nirvana.

As a pup, Sophie approximated this by leaping upon birds drawn to our water sprinkler and enthusiastically shaking them to actual pieces. As she has aged out of the killer demographic, however, she has learned to find her pleasures elsewhere. The beach is one such place, but not because seagulls call forth memory of blood and water. She is not the hunter she once was and I am not naive.

I know only too well that the reason our furry friend goes wild at the first whisper of crashing surf is that she is already imagining the giddy joy of befouling herself at water's edge. For this reason I will normally walk Sophie for an hour before we get to the beach. And I take her at different times of day, lest she determine a pattern to our outings and set herself the challenge of holding bowel and bladder tight until some innocent child's carefully constructed and much-loved sandcastle presents itself as a tempting target for explosive discharge.

No. We walk and we walk the hot, dusty backstreets until she has done her dirty business and it is safe to have her off the leash near sand and water.

Or so I thought, until yesterday. A full hour I gave

her on the lead, with multiple breaks to make potty and water the parched and yellow grass of Byron's less travelled byways. When at last it seemed there could be nothing left, no chance of being disgraced in public, we repaired to the surf.

A fine hot day it was, with a lovely rolling swell peeling north of the small rocky outcrop that marked the edge of the sanctioned area where dogs might play and frolic. Many children were about, watched over by their parents, and many other dogs too. All behaving and enjoying themselves.

I let slip the hound, who bolted after a border collie and took to racing back and forth up and down the beach, a pleasing sight after recent woes and injuries. We carefully chose the breeder from whom we took our pup. Frank Meusberger, a retired copper, was a thoughtful and conservative breeding master. He had never sought to produce the highly prized and hugely expensive brown labs you see on rare occasions. Force-breeding that particular strain brings out the genetic errors which can torment older labradors with hip problems.

Sophie when young was a small but sturdy animal, strong and fit. She maintained her fitness even as the years piled up on her, but she had of late been bothered by arthritis. It was a pleasure then to see her move so freely and with such vigour on the sand.

Not that I allowed my normal vigilance to slip. A close watch I kept, lest she suddenly begin to display the telltale signs of a dog in search of a dumping spot. One can never be too careful.

There was no warning.

After running about for ten minutes, with no sign of needing to take a canine comfort break, she suddenly charged into a small lagoon-like area in front of a number of families, and panting and smiling in that way that dogs do, she let loose with an enormous and distressing explosion of semi-liquid brown spray, carrying within it the lumps of heavier, more solid matter.

It was as though time ceased to have meaning. A small bubble of suspended reality enclosed that whole beach. Waves no longer crashed. Gulls no longer soared. The other dogs all ceased their ceaseless charging about.

All was still.

And then one child, downstream of the toxic event, screamed.

And then all the children screamed, their parents yelled, and I roared at the dog to stop what she was doing. All of this naturally served only to reward her with the sort of attention that demanded even more panting and spraying and bounding about.

I was moving towards the contaminated site, slowly at first, in disbelief, but accelerating as the horror of it dawned on me. The children were quickly moving away, often hauled out of the sea by cursing parents who could not have splashed more water about had they been trying to secure their charges from a Great White.

The dog, meanwhile, who seemed to have stored a week's worth of bodily wastes in a secret place for just this moment, continued to leap and spray and turn in circles. I had my phone in one hand held high above my head, a doo-doo bag in the other and the eyes of everyone upon me as I raced towards the deposits to somehow scoop them up. Also racing towards them was an unusually large set of waves. Great fantails of water arced up behind me as I accelerated. Sophie barked in joy at such a jolly caper. Parents and surfers did not.

The waves made it there before I did, scattering and atomising everything, while I traipsed forlornly back and forth making a sad, pathetic show of launching myself at anything that looked even vaguely brown and collectible.

How long does one stay in the water and show willing under such circumstances?

For as long as anyone who witnessed your original disgrace remains.

We were a long time getting out of the shallows of shame.

cheeseburgergothic.com, September 2012

We would become Volvo drivers

There's no avoiding death and taxes, but surely I could give the Volvo station wagon a swerve? No, said my good lady wife. We had a new baby and that meant life as we knew it was over. No more nude surfing. No more Xbox drinking games. (Master Chief gets stuck in a doorway? Drink!) And no more fun cars.

Her little Mini, a perfect student car, which four hefty blokes could flip over onto its roof for an impromptu game of spin the bottle when all the actual bottles were still busy providing a home for my home-brew? Gone.

My dream of crossing the continent in a retooled Hilux powered by the concentrated leftovers from the bottom of the home-brew barrel? Gone.

No, it was time for the boxy Nordic dependability and to hell with the humiliation. We would become Volvo drivers. And just to tighten and accelerate the shame spiral, that'd be a station wagon, the extra space invaluable for hauling fold-up cots, a small zoo of stuffed animals wrapped in a Barbie blanket and giant bundles of nappies all secured by the last lingering threads of my street cred and fast-fading awesomeness.

The V60 it was we drove off the lot, in a stealthy shade of metallic grey, the colour of leaden skies and stolid, enforced rectitude. Instantly I felt like filing my taxes and cleaning out the gutters at home.

We lived at Bondi in those days, where the lack of off-street parking spilled a bright, gleaming riot of cars out into the clean salt air. Soft tops, convertibles, Combis, shaggin' wagons, and the muscular SUVs favoured by those many members of the Russian mafia who had recently escaped the former Soviet Union for our groovy beachside village … Oh and our sturdy grey family transport option, of course. It was also parked out on the street overlooking the famous bay.

Did the high incidence of car theft in the suburb bother us? Professional gangs of 'rebirthers' were often drawn to Bondi, where they hid in the massive tidal flows of tourists. But no, that did not bother us, for we were Volvo owners. Not only was our choice of motor so determinedly unhip that it threatened whiplash as potential car thieves shook their heads in horror at the very thought of making off with it, but the cunning Swedes had fitted our vehicle with one of the first digital immobiliser systems.

It would not be stolen, they promised.

And so it was not, until the day some villain put a brick through the front window and stole it anyway. Perhaps there were no WRXs around.

It was a drag, a massive drag in fact, but we were insured and the cops were helpful, assuring us we could forget about ever seeing the car, nappies or Barbie blanket again as they stamped and signed their report for the insurer.

And then things turned to custard. Swedish custard, made by the Muppets' Swedish chef. So fiercely did Volvo insist that this car could not have been stolen with their immobiliser fitted that the insurance company began to have its doubts. I had visions of the Swedish chef 'strudel-oodle-oodling' down the phone at some dubious assessor, becoming more and more agitated at the idea their perfect system had failed.

'Ooodle doodle noodle Börmoongoon oodle stool üt.'

Luckily the thoughtful car thieves thoughtfully stole some more 'immobilised' Volvos, or maybe the cops convinced my insurance company of just how good our car thieves were, because they eventually paid up.

Allowing us to buy another Volvo.

Wheels, May 2013

'This car's from the future!'

And so a ten-year-old boy cuts to the heart of it. My son, who thinks nothing of holding a small glass plate in his hand and talking to his Uncle Bill on the far side of the planet, via a better video link than the IT desk on the Death Star could serve up for Lord Vader, gasped with delight at the sci-fi hum of Holden's Volt the first time I pressed the ignition. The opalescent blue glow of the start light helped with the suspension of disbelief too.

Disbelief in his case that he was actually going to get to ride, Skywalker-style, in something that felt like a hover car. And a slightly naggier concern in mine that perhaps the car wasn't actually turned on yet. The sonorous hum was supposed to assure me that we were good for lift-off, but the spooky lack of any engine vibration, or growl, the absence of that reassuring magic-fingers butt massage I enjoyed for so many years when nursing a trembling Renault through late-stage dementia, seemed to imply that nothing had happened beyond sound effects and a rather modest light show.

But a slight press on the accelerator and away we glided, into the future. A future of bumped chins and neck strain, at times, but undeniably someplace where everybody would one day wear silver bodysuits and eat astronaut food.

In the week we had the loaner from Holden, I never quite grew accustomed to feeling that we'd engaged the anti-grav drive and were floating a few inches above the tarmac, rather than rolling over the bitumen, although the Volt did its best to break the fantasy by bottoming out on every driveway we encountered. It was annoying enough that I began to plan parking strategies ten minutes out from every destination, lest I have to return it with the sort of damage you'd get leading with your chin against Georges St-Pierre.

The neck strain was a function of having to crane around for visibility in an otherwise very comfortably appointed cabin that felt at times like the inside of an APC. A very toney and luxe APC to be sure, but one with niggardly firing slits out of which to keep an eye on your road enemies.

Between them, these quibbles, both easily fixed, amounted to pretty much my only problems with the Volt. Other than some initial nervousness as the first battery charge dropped towards zero during peak hour – eventually cutting out in the middle of Brisbane's Story Bridge – Holden's big bet on the eco-car market was a joy to behold. The battery is good for about 70 klicks of city work and transitions seamlessly to the back-up petrol-electric engine when you've sucked the last drop of juice from it. With a full tank your range stretches out to more than 600 kilometres.

But, if you've ever stood despairing at a petrol pump as your kiddies' college fund gets pumped into the treasure vaults of the Saudi royal family, you will love, love, love the feeling of getting one back on the Middle East as you plug your car into a stock standard wall socket in the garage and power up. This was an especially pleasing experience for me, having just installed solar panels the week before. Pretty much everywhere we drove the Volt, we did so powered by the sun. The world's most tedious super-hippy could not have been more pleased with himself had he found a way to knit Birkenstocks out of alfalfa muffins.

Was it fun to fly? Hells yes! There was more than enough power here to hold our own on the freeway, and no sense of drag when it came to giving the warp engines a nudge. The Volt won't have the electric vehicle market to itself, of course. But after a week spent in the future with it, I was, like my boy, keenly wondering, 'Are we there yet, are we there yet?'

Wheels, May 2013

MODERN MAN

Manspreading

Gentlemen, prepare yourselves.

We are at war and we face the final assault on the last bastion of the sole surviving freedom left to a man. Yes, gentlemen, the battle of the bulge is upon us. The misandrist forces have concentrated in a painful pincer movement and hit us where it hurts the most.

The manspreading war has begun.

We have confirmed reports from the American front of two men arrested on the subway for doing nothing more than God intended when God packed all our dangly bits where they would quickly be crushed without due care and attention being paid to the provision of ample *Lebensraum*.

The so-called Police Reform Organizing Project (PROP – which sounds to me very much like some sort of Clementine Ford–approved Kickstarter for ruining everybody's fun) reports: 'Police officers arrested two Latino men on the charge of "manspreading" on the subway', apparently because they were history's greatest monsters for 'taking up more than one seat and therefore inconveniencing other riders'.

Well thanks for that, Clem, but allow me to mansplain.

While it is possible that a certain sort of fellow, the sort, let's say, who wears lumpy jumpers and eats roughage muffins by choice, might find it biologically plausible to sit for more than two minutes with legs closed like a small convent schoolgirl, every other single man in the whole world would be, well, unmanned by such a preposterous demand on his anatomy.

It is just not possible.

Our boys need to roam free.

It is not simply a matter of individual convenience – although, let me say, there is nothing more inconvenient and uncomfortable to a fellow than having his boys penned in when all they want to do in the world is gallop forth like noble stallions on the wide open prairies of possibility. Bad enough that we are forced by convention to tightly swaddle them in the strict and unnatural constraints of the modern underpant – a poor substitute for the swirling kilts, roomy togas and hypo-allergenic oak leaves of manly antiquity, let me tell you. But that we should now not even presume to afford our little folk the dignity and repose of just a little extra wiggle room … it is intolerable.

What is to become of humanity if Man is not able to spread wherever he damned well pleases? It is the destiny of mankind to spread out across the stars and, as needs be, across all available seating space on any public transport to the aforementioned stars.

Gentlemen, I put it to you that here we must make our stand while sitting down and spreading out just enough to make things comfortable. If they take this from us what do we have left besides all the power and money and privilege?

brisbanetimes.com.au, June 2015

Without pants

I understand. It's hot. And in the heat and the steam-press humidity a fellow sometimes feels the need to loosen the tie, undo the top button, perhaps to even let out the strides a little so his boys can breathe. I understand that. I'm a writer. I work from home. Most days pants are entirely optional.

But most days I don't leave home. And if I do feel the need for the delicate kiss of fresh air on derrière, in deference to others I will not drop pants until I am completely alone. Even the dog should not have to deal with that sort of thing. (Rugby League professionals, take note.)

It was with eyes wide and mouth agape, then, that I found myself in Byron Bay confronted by a fellow, who was not a writer, who had assumed for himself the author's privilege of going about his business all but starkers. I say all but, because this six-and-a-half, maybe seven-foot tall Byron identity, was shod, but only shoddily.

He wore only a frayed and moth-eaten pair of shorts on his long and rangy frame – all elbows, knees, knobbly backbone, stringy blond mullet and pubic hair. Acres and acres of it, bursting over the top of these terrible shorts like an old-growth forest run wild on plutonium fertiliser. And from that horrifying state of nature grew one thick-trunked ghost gum, mercifully hidden for most of its length, but not all, by the thin scraps of old KingGee he had pulled on that morning before heading to the chicken shack.

For that is where he found us and all the other horrified customers, at our repast, attempting to eat delicious white meat, when suddenly confronted by the prospect of his hairy and entirely unappetising white meat attempting to escape from its insecure and not-so-secret containment facility.

One hardly knew where to look. Mostly deep into one's double chicken burger, as it turned out.

The situation did not much improve after Creepy McNastypants slid on by with a hugely self-satisfied smirk on his dial, for the arse end of his inadequate shorts were ripped from top to bottom, inviting the unwary to lose themselves in there as they considered the crack of doom.

Was it a power trip? Did I just get flashed while necking my double chicken burger? Is it that we must accept when visiting freak shows like Byron Bay that the occasional freak will show more of themselves than is really necessary?

I don't know. But it really put me right off my schnitzel.

brisbanetimes.com.au, February 2016

Cold snap

You people are soft. First hint of frost on the air and you're all wearing four layers of Snuggies to work and Ugg boots on your wobbly bits before lining up around the corner at The Dark Chocolatier for all the brownies and hot chocolates.

Well back off, wussies.

All your brownies belong to me now.

I earned them.

I'm writing this nude. On my deck. In the wind. Because I can. And just let me say … no shrinkage. I am unimpressed with this so-called Antarctic vortex, let me tell you. When I were a lad, growing up in Ipswich, the Siberia of Queensland, we would laugh at your so-called low temperatures, worthless Brisbane weaklings. Laugh, I tell you, because inappropriately excited Christian Brothers made us stand out in the cold, nude, and would flog us with extension cords every time we shivered.

So we learned not to shiver.

And I do not shiver now, the same way I did not

shiver when walking to and from school in the teeth of winter, uphill both ways, barefoot, while carrying a heavy sack full of frozen cane toads for teacher.

And you reckon you feel cold this week.

Everyone reckons they feel cold this week.

'I tell my kids how I had to pry my hands off the handlebars of my bike when I got to school in Toowoomba – and that was with no gloves on,' my editor tells me when I tell him I'm going to write how soft everyone is about the cold. 'I'd ride up this hill, but couldn't see the top for the fog, with sleet blowing straight in my face through the hole in my balaclava, stalactites forming on the end of my nose. Yes, I wore a balaclava.'

'Fucking soft,' I said.

The only balaclava I had was stripped from the frozen popsicle of a robber who wasn't quick enough getting from his getaway panel van to the door of the Ipswich and West Moreton Building Society. And I only took his balaclava so I could throw it away because balaclavas are soft.

We didn't need no lousy balaclavas in Ipswich. If you absolutely had to protect your precious and delicate complexion from the screaming banshee winds howling in off the frozen slushy of the Bremer River, you simply cut a make-do mask from the hairy arse of any weaklings who froze to death in the absolute zero which is the mean maximum temperature of a mild winter's day in Ipswich even as global warming threatens to bake the planet to a crisp.

So STFU, Brisbane, about being so cold. And leave one of those brownies for me.

brisbanetimes.com.au, July 2015

Bachelor pad

There was a time when, like all men, I dreamed James Bond dreams of bachelorhood. Dreams of black dinner jackets and dry martinis, of high-rise apartments with sunken lounge pits and Olympic-sized hot tubs in which frolicked an endless parade of giddy blonde female weather presenters. A designer vision of Lone Wolf Nirvana.

The wolf's den sat in the centre of this vision. The perfect batch pad of the imagination, a lotus trap for the hundreds of doe-eyed bimbos who would find the lure of its lava lamps and deep shag pile carpets completely irresistible. I imagined wining and dining them out on the terrazzo. Dizzying them with my masterful command of half a dozen regional cooking styles. Plying them with obscure little numbers from my collection of vintage Champagnes. Wondering how long it would take to get them out of that low-cut Versace cocktail dress and into my evil clutches.

All in heroic defiance of the fact that for most men being a bachelor means sitting at home alone, watching *Star Trek* reruns and late-night information-als as a big dollop of chilli con carne and sour cream lands on your unwashed Homer Simpson T-shirt. You scoop it up with a spoon, look at the stain and wonder, 'Hmm, how long is that gonna take to wear out?'

Sadly, young men – the only men possessed of the physical stamina needed to really do the bache-lor life justice – are generally always short of both the cash and, more importantly, the social graces needed to bring off the act with any style. I am reminded of a guileless young country guy who, having unexpect-edly tumbled some daughter of the landed gentry into his bedroll, was taken aback to discover she had morphed into a sexually carnivorous hellcat demand-ing he 'talk dirty' to her. Thirty seconds of hot, embar-rassed silence ensued before he could bring himself to cough, 'Aargh … The price of greasy wool was really shit this year.'

Is it any wonder that the average bachelor tends to spend a lot more time with other bachelors than with women? In other words, with his natural compet-itors rather than his natural prey? Because, while prey they may be, idiots they are not. Like twitchy gazelles sniffing the danger wafting from a pack of mangy, pot-bellied old cougars, smart women approach the bachelor's lair with ears pricked, nostrils flared and getaway routes planned well in advance. This wariness is even more pronounced when advancing on a group of males sharing the same house, cave or hollowed-out tree stump. The last bachelor house I shared in, we had three women visit in 18 months, not counting our mothers. And, perhaps put off by the half-chewed Big Mac steadfastly refusing to decompose atop the TV set throughout those 18 months, none ever made a return visit.

Some men, sensing the ineffectiveness of traditional bachelor role models, attempted to subvert this paradise. Hence, throughout the '80s and early '90s we were subjected to snags. Not the delicious crumbed variety available from any butcher for a very reasonable price. The other sort. The ones we don't like to talk about any more because it's a bit embarrassing for all concerned. The sensitive, lumpy jumper-loving foot-rub specialists, who turned away from their brothers, moved out on their own and started inviting the womenfolk around for home-cooked dinners, only to present them with an earthen mug of hideous, non-alcoholic beetroot wine and a couple of home-baked roughage muffins, with no sugar or chocolate or anything, only love to hold together a handful of rolled oats and shrubbery. No, we won't talk about them.

Well, maybe a bit. Because for all of their smiley-faced vacuousness, the snags got one thing right. Lone wolves have to operate on their own. When I realised this I moved out of the year-round party house scene and made for the beach. Checked out the seaside villages up and down the east coast. Figured I might settle into one as a sort of Lone Wolf writer-in-residence. My house would be on a headland with a wooden deck out the front and a white beach curving into the sea mist like a scimitar lying in the morning sun. I'd be up early, running along the beach and returning to a breakfast of fruit salad and black coffee, prepared by Miko, my enigmatic and beautiful Japanese housemaid. There would be rumours about us in town. I'd probably hit the typewriter at 11 o'clock. You would hear my old black Underwood start up like sporadic gunfire in a bad neighbourhood. Later I'd walk comfortably through the town's covert, vigorous Latin Quarter where night roared to tequila-fuelled bar fights, vendettas and card games, where handcarts, stray dogs and snake sellers wound their way through Russian transvestites, Mexican sailors and drunken two-fisted warrior poets on the lookout for cheap whores and broken hearts. I would have the rich, heady hash cake of bachelorhood and I would eat it too.

Sadly, things didn't turn out that way. For one thing, Porpoise Spit had no covert but vigorous Latin Quarter. And then I did have a lot of TV to catch up on. And some bastard set up a delivery service which brought beer and pizza right to your banana lounge.

And the laundromat was just a bit too far away to get my Homer Simpson T-shirt washed every month. And ... you can guess the rest.

No martinis. No weather girls. No hot tubs or dinner jackets.

But at least I hear that next month the pizza place is offering two Supremes for the price of one. Maybe I could get a few of the dudebros over.

The Independent Monthly, July 1994

The Tasmanian Babes fiasco

The most fucked-up night of my life ended like this. I spilled through the Tasmanians' front door, pants around my ankles, howling like a loon. I caught my foot on something and went down. But it didn't matter because I felt no pain. I was so far gone by then I couldn't tell up from down. The world seemed to swim up to me through a watery red mist and all I could make out through this mist were a lot of very serious looking people. Then the mushroom-farm delivery van exploded out on the Babes' front lawn. This was a piss-poor turn of events, which I feel compelled to set down here in the hope that others might avoid the same ruinous folly.

I'm not sure which domino fell first. The Babes? The Thunderbird? The mountain of drugs and tequila? I just don't know. Trying to get this straight is a bit like pushing blocks of coloured smoke around my head. But I blame it all on the Tasmanian Babes. So we might as well start with them.

There were three of them. Three Tasmanian

babes. A tall one with big brown hair and cowboy boots; a short, huge one with a spray of freckles on her nose. And the other one, a blonde who liked to get around in bare feet and chew gum a lot. I forget their names. They were working their way around the country and had fetched up in a house just up the street from my place. They were new in town, didn't know too many people and they were all a little bit dim.

This Thunderbird I mention, his name was Ron. Thunderbird Ron. We called him that because he'd gotten into bodybuilding, and I mean really gotten into it. He'd grown so huge and monstrous that he moved around like a badly strung puppet, the way those guys do, like they've got so much muscle and bulk on them their arms stick out from their sides and they don't seem able to bring their knees together when they walk. His personality was sort of stiff and wooden too and he had a stilted way of talking, as though he had to bench press his own weight to squeeze out the words. He knocked back about ten gallons of this really foul wheatgerm- and egg-based protein drink every day and watched an unhealthy number of early Schwarzenegger videos, but he was alright. He could pick up a lounge chair with his teeth, which was useful sometimes. He also had a problem with women. They terrified him. This came home to me one day —

literally – when I was sitting in the lounge room playing on the Box of X.

The Thunderbird waddled in, really agitated. I glanced up and noticed right off that he had this big white bandage wrapped around his hand, but I didn't pay it much heed. Figured he must've crushed it between some dumbbells down the gym or something. I said, 'Howdy,' and turned back to the game. Thing was though, I just couldn't concentrate because Ron was looming over me putting out the psychic waves of borderline panic. I blew off the game, leaned back from the console and asked what the trouble was. He wanted to know if I could give him some advice on nightclubbing clothes, which is a laugh if you know me. I wear rotting T-shirts with advertising slogans on them. But the Thunderbird ploughed on regardless, explained in this tortured passage of dialogue that he wanted to go to a nightclub to 'meet some women who he might be able to have some sex with'.

I thought, no way man! Never happen. I explained that those sorts of places, they weren't for him. They were terrible places, a bit like black holes, except they collapsed in on themselves under the weight of their own bad vibes. The idea of Ron in one of those places, it just didn't sit right. I tried to talk him out of the idea but it was 1000 miles of hard road. He was locked in and tracking. He was hot guns on the whole thing.

He'd gone and got this Mr Universe physique, worked hard for it, suffered for it, and now it was time to go out and get some sex because women, 'they wouldn't have had a chance to have sex with a man like me before'.

I thought, Thunderbird, you speak the truth.

I was getting a little keen to change the topic so I said he didn't look like he was up to much at that moment on account of the bandage he was sporting. Asked whether he'd broken his wrist at the gym, knowing that if I could get him onto the gym he'd talk for hours about carbo-loading and steroid abuse and reps and sets and all that shit, perhaps even forgetting about sex altogether. At least that's what I thought. But when I mentioned the bandage he became even more cramped and downshifted than before. Explained he'd broken all these bones in his hand the other day when the blonde Tasmanian girl from across the road, the barefoot, gum-chewing, space alien beauty queen, had smiled at him in the street. And he'd wanted to talk to her. He'd been burning to talk to her, in fact he wanted to ask her out to a nightclub, but he couldn't, he just couldn't, she smiled at him, and said hello, and he'd … and she'd … and … and … and …

So he'd scuttled inside, made a fist and punched out the wall in the hallway.

Okay, that was cool. There had been some talk

about the appearance of that mysterious giant cavity.
And I did have some sympathy with this poor bastard
standing in front of me, sweating and squirming and
generally looking like all of his vital bodily fluids had
backed up and he was maybe three seconds away from
rolling his eyes, sprouting thick, matted clumps of fur
on his palms and punching into the nearest warm hole
he could find.

You see, I knew all about the barefoot one. I myself
had been smiled at in the street, just one day previous.
But unlike the T-bird I had bounded over like a horny
little puppy and made ready to do the nasty right then
and there, in broad daylight in the middle of the street.

She had smiled at me, after all. But when I got
there, she said with a smirk of an arch conspirator,
'Your friend, the gym guy, he's a big boy, isn't he?'

'Oh yeah,' I smiled, slightly deflated but not wanting to show it. 'All natural too, won't have a bar of
them 'roids.'

'You know, you guys should come over,' she said.
'We're having a housewarming on Saturday.'

'You're sure? All of us?' I asked.

'Whatever,' she said. 'Just be sure and bring
He-Man with you.'

You bet, I'd said, and wandered off, mental cogs
spinning and whirring at full speed. The thing was,
when word got out that the Tasmanian Babes were

throwing a party there would be no question of non-attendance. The house would go ballistic. Come the first rustle of a Doritos packet or the pop of a Spumante bottle there be a stampede, a thunderous phalanx of lusty, beer-crazed youths spilling down the front steps of our house and charging up the road like one of those angry cartoon clouds with a riot of arms and legs and bolts of lightning exploding from it. But, it seemed, we were dependent on the T-Bird's doubtful charisma for our entry. There was only one thing for it. House meeting.

'Excellent!'

'Fantastic!'

'Outstanding!' they went, just like a Pepsi ad.

'I dunno,' muttered Thunderbird, deep in the grip of a Maximum Fear.

'Just wear your posing pouch and a pair of sandals,' somebody suggested.

The house was gathered around an ugly-looking pile of glistening grey bones and soiled refresher towels. It had been a bucket of the Colonel's finest, but that was a long time ago, in a galaxy far, far away. I licked the rich greasy scum of secret herbs and additives from my fingers, already regretting my third Kentucky Fried Mistake that month. I told the guys about the party and about the T-Bird's extraordinary luck.

They were a mixed bunch in this house. There

was myself, not doing much of anything at that point. The T-Bird, of course. Elroy, who delivered milk in a van and styled himself as the Milko from Acapulco, even though he was from Rooty Hill. There was Brainthrust Leonard, a gawky, third-year engineering student with an unrivalled back catalogue of *Star Trek* fanzines and tentacle porn. And in the room next to Leonard lived Jabba the Hutt, who watched so much television that his hair fused with the mouldering fabric of the brown couch, forcing him to live by the remote control, because if he'd ever actually got up off the couch he'd have had to walk around with a couple of filthy, rotting cushions stuck to his arse like the Post-it notes of a Lesser God.

A fold-up cot in the living room was home to Mick, our very own English soccer hooligan. Mick liked to travel around the world and headbutt things. We'd had one woman in the house, a Japanese traveller by the name of Satomi Tiger. But when she left we became an all-male house. We went full dudebro when Brainthrust Leonard announced that he liked to sit on his hands before a wank with his tentacle porn, because his fingers went numb and then it felt 'just like baby Cthulhu'. That led to a chorus of salty yarns and masturbatory oneupmanship, I can tell you. It reached a low point with Mick's demonstration of penile push-ups – a ludicrous exercise which involved draping a wet bath towel over his erect member and repeatedly raising and lowering it like a boom gate.

You can imagine how these barbarians reacted to the invite from the Tasmanian Babes. There wasn't a man among us who didn't think himself the object of those women's lustful intentions, except for the T-Bird of course, and that huge tongue-tied baboon with the pudding-bowl haircut was the only one of us who was actually in with a chance.

The party didn't kick off until seven or eight in the evening, and we planned to hit the ground running. We'd agreed that those who intended to go to the Babes' party had a responsibility to ensure that it really was the ugliest, most debauched and bestial orgy these hotties would ever encounter. To that end we had fanned out through the city, each of us shaking the trees of our various underworld contacts, dislodging a pharmacological cornucopia and, judging by the number of people now crammed into our kitchen, picking up a fair number of camp followers along the way.

There were dozens of people and all had arrived bearing bags of smoke. Some generous souls had also tossed in a few sheets of acid, a little ecstasy, and, I'm sorry to add, a whole case of really cheap, vile, generic brand tequila. Old El Gringo or something like that. The sort with a dead plastic scorpion bumping around down the bottom of the bottle. It was an impressive haul, which held the room in a quiet, almost reverent sort of thrall for a while. Most impressive of all, however, was the dope mountain on the kitchen table. You really had to be there and lay eyes on the sucker to believe such a marvel could have existed. As it grew and grew it reduced everyone to excited giggles, then to whispers, and finally to awed and simple silence. It was maybe two feet across at the base, a rough circle climbing to chest height from the table top, a rich green tangle, a mound of pot wound through with long, tightly compressed sticky buds and knots of purple heads.

It was maybe 3.30 in the afternoon by then. Hours to go before the party. Hours to sit there, staring at the dope mountain, waiting for the cops to crash in through the windows and cut us down with tear gas and karate chops and a few bursts of submachine gun fire.

'Let's just smoke the fucking thing,' said Mick.

And we fell on it.

***

I awoke hours later, on the brown couch, surrounded by hundreds of people. The house was roaring. I was still stoned, but it wasn't the trippy, free-falling pleasant sort of stone which had rushed on after my third cone of the afternoon. It was a heavy, slouchy, turn your brain to trickle sort of stone. I pushed through the crowd, making my way to the kitchen, hoping to toke up and take off again. But when I got there ... The table was bare. I shook my head. I remembered that there had been so much shit to get through that we had stopped bothering with single joints. People were just ripping handfuls of ganja out of the pile and stuffing them into improvised cones and bongs and corncob pipes. I remembered being so wasted my vision had started to come apart, the colours and lines melting into each other. And then I woke up on the couch.

People were hanging out of the windows and partying in the mango trees out the front. There were cars all over the garden. Punters kept rolling in, and I was swept along by this whirling, thunderous, clamouring mob; this sweating, seething tide of unwashed dreads and shiny shaven domes, of torn jeans, yellow teeth, hipster beards, Apache girls with Zulu spears, henna tatts and Celtic runes; this savage caterwauling crush of human flux and flow which pressed in hard upon the mind until time itself broke up and swirled around in little lost jigsaw moments of disintegrated continuity.

A voice screamed in my ear, 'Get on the end of this one.'

It was Mick, with a doobie the size of a Cuban cigar, wrapped in bright pink paper. I shouted thanks and toked up, drawing the rich, acrid smoke down, letting it smooth my jagged edges and take me deep. I asked what had happened. He misunderstood, I think, and tried to tell me some story in his impenetrable English accent about feeding some young Catholic schoolgirl a trip. He'd found her at the terminal point of completely self-indulgent realistic drunkenness, swaying and drinking and talking to herself about how nasty the world was. Mick had thought a tab might cheer her up. But she'd just greedily gobbled it down and disappeared. Hours later Braintrust Leonard had found her standing in front of a full-length window on the verandah, holding the hem of her skirt out and twirling from side to side like a little girl. As he was watching, her face turned feral and she punched out the window, left a big spider web of cracks in it, then turned around, saw them and freaked.

They tried putting the soothers on her but she escaped by grabbing a small piece of rubber tubing sticking down from the gutter and trying to swing away like Catwoman. It broke and she fell to the driveway with a big sick splat, but jumped right up and ran away. Nobody saw her again but the phone kept ringing all night. It was her, but all she ever said was, 'no way out no way out no way out stop' then she hung up.

Mick was upset about the waste of his tab but he was determined to put it behind him on a river of tequila. I found the shaven-headed lunatic in the kitchen, waving quickly gathered fistfuls of Old El Gringo and cackling like a fiend bent on certain self-destruction.

Even in my advanced stage of moral decay I shouted inwardly at the prospect of hopping into this evil-looking toxic waste. It had a greasy, pissy colour, vaguely reminiscent of the ancient dusty jars lining the cabinets of my old high-school science lab, jars of dark yellow saline in which floated the flaky, slightly rotten bodies of long-dead tiger snakes and miscarried kitten foetuses. My stomach rolled over slowly at the thought. Tequila and I did not have a good history. The last time our paths had crossed – an ugly, senseless binge to celebrate Mexico's national day – I'd been forced to spend 33 hours spread-eagled on a polished wooden floor, convinced I'd been nailed there, so great was the pain which spiked through all my joints and organs.

Still, you know, a drink's a drink, so we fetched some lemonade from the fridge and three plastic Ronald McDonald glasses from the dish rack and set about lining up and knocking down a full set of Old El Gringo slammers. And an awful, terrible fighting business it was too. Apart from Mekong Delta whiskey and some obscure brands of Ukrainian cabbage vodka, tequila is the only drink I know that acts as a genuine stimulant. Bang bang bang went the slammers, sending frothy eruptions of alcoholic lemonade over the rim of our glasses before exploding like sickly sweet hand grenades behind the thin dome of bone holding our sorry, fucked-up brains in place.

Then Mick remembered that we had another party to go to.

The Babes!

I roared so loud at the memory that I hurt my lungs and had to sit down for a while. Then I was off, fucked, hysterical, crashing up the hallway towards my room with my jeans down around my ankles, intent on changing for their party. The tequila, the smoke and the lust all combined and sparked in a high-octane, dangerously unstable mix which licked like fire at the base of my brain stem and seemed to cause a distant, fearful roar. I fell through the door, hitting the wall and leaving a huge dent there. A couple of Eurotrash travellers were thrashing around in my bed, but I ignored them and they me. I was so completely uncoordinated I couldn't get my jeans on or off. I simply rolled around on the floor, hysterical and spinning out.

Mick stuck his head in to yell that he and Elroy were taking the milk van and going as 'the fucking peppers'. I had no idea what he was talking about, but I didn't want them getting there first, so I shucked up my pants as best I could and staggered out after them, barrelling through half a dozen strangers sitting on our front steps. I caught a flash of Mick's naked butt before he climbed into the mushroom van and the headlights blinded me. I ran. They drove.

The Babes' place was only two or three doors up from ours, but I beat them because they crashed into our mailbox on the way. I hit the Babes' door at full tilt and, like I said, crashed to the floor with my pants around my ankles. The horrified partygoers – there were a few of them, very intense looking folk, like in an opera box with martini glasses and little nibbly snacks held between their pinkies and thumbs – well, they had no time to react to my grand entrance, because my roommates were bringing up the rear.

Mick and Elroy careened across the lawn like suicide bombers with the van's headlights on high beam and the Red Hot Chili Peppers cranked up to the max on Elroy's boom box. The Peppers had been in town just the week before and Mick had seen them do their socks-on-cocks routine. They had also worn space helmets with flames coming out, so Mick and Elroy, fans that they were, had been laying plans to emulate them ever since. That afternoon they had stolen a couple of plastic witches hats from some nearby roadworks. They soaked rolled-up newspapers in petrol, jammed them into the hole at the top and left the lot sitting in the van for a few hours. Then, as I was rolling around on the floor of my room, they had both stripped naked, grabbed a sock, and attached them to their willies with rubber bands before charging out to the van.

They mounted the gutter, kicking the spotlights to full beam and smashing through a picket fence. They jumped out and lit up their hats, forgetting that the van was full of petrol fumes. There was a massive flash explosion – WHOOF! – and then Mick and Elroy were the ass-kicking Chili Peppers no more. No. They were just a couple of fools running around with socks on their cocks and their heads on fire. I was trampled as the guests ran to put them out.

They weren't allowed to stay at the housewarming party and neither was I, so we all went home. The party kicked on until four or five in the morning. I had a few more joints and remembered becoming convinced I could defuse my atoms through the structure of the house by sheer willpower. I don't remember spending the better part of the night on my hands and knees butting my head up against the lounge room wall until I passed out. But people tell me that I did.

Duffy and Snellgrove, 1998

Manflu

Women? Pfft! They're all sniffling malingerers. And scientists have proven it with science. Manflu science. And they were male scientists, too, of course. The lady scientists are disputing the results, as they would. Because they've denied for years that the accursed winter curse even exists. Now they feel bad about not bringing us our Lemsip and fluffing up the pillows like we asked while we just checked the TV schedule.

Men scientists from the University of Newcastle's FluTracking program have proven that because men are much harder than women, our manflu bugs are also much tougher and not to be trifled with at all, even though they don't deign to even bother with the ladies, who aren't much of a challenge to their lethal deadliness. Some lady scientists disagree, but, whatever.

Analysis of more than 16 000 FluTracking survivors from last year has found that 'Women took an average of 3 days off normal duties with cough and fever, whereas men took an average of *only 2.8 days off!*' (Italics, exclamation mark and the word 'only' added to show you just how serious this situation is.) What's more, 'among those ill enough to visit an emergency department, women took an average of *a whole lazy 4 days off*, whereas men took only 3.5 days off' and were very brave about it too. (Again with the extra italics and possibly the words 'whole' and 'lazy', which I thought I'd better add just in case there were some women of low calibre about who weren't taking this manflu crisis seriously.)

The man scientists and their lab ladies split along gender lines when interpreting the results, which showed very clearly that 'the decreased duration of illness among males with cough and fever visiting an emergency department could represent stoicism', and not, as otherwise claimed, that men 'were more likely to present to an emergency department with milder illness'.

Men, of course, don't present anywhere when they have manflu. They just die, manfully. (Notice how closely related those words are? Manflu. Manful. That's not an accident.)

I've been dying of it all week and can hardly type this column because of the Niagara of snot pouring down my face and the painful fires of a thousand suns burning in my joints and muscles, which being manly muscles are able to carry a much heavier load of pain than lady muscles.

So we'll hear no more of 'mythical manflu' this winter. Science has spoken. And now that science has finally settled this question, I would like a hot rum toddy, thanks, love.

brisbanetimes.com.au, May 2013

Dad bod

Step aside, CrossFit nazis. Back off, gym junkies. I got what ladies want, and it's not your grotesque angular deformities. The internet has spoken. Or one chick with a blog, or something, has written, and the internet has gone mad for it and, anyway, bottom line … Make way for the dad bod.

It's been around for a while. I've had mine for about 15 years. But it's only in the last month or so that the dad bod has made its way from campus whispers onto the radar of the mainstream press via an essay by American college girl Mackenzie Pearson, 'Why Girls Love the Dad Bod'.

Pearson lets the wider world in on a poorly held secret. The ladies are all about the dad bod. 'The dad bod is a nice balance between a beer gut and working out. The dad bod says, "I go to the gym occasionally, but I also drink heavily on the weekends and enjoy eating eight slices of pizza at a time."'

If Pearson doesn't get a Pulitzer for this, journalism is dead. Why, just last week I almost went to the gym, I drank heavily, and this very morning there were a number of pizza slices in my fridge. Now there are not.

Desperate trend-hopping mediavores were all over the dad bod like an extra-roomy pair of trackies. 'Apparently, women are very into them,' mused *GQ*.

'Can we talk about dad bod sex?' asked Stella Bugbee (not a made-up name), editorial director of The Cut (not a made-up lady website).

Why yes, Ms Bugbee. Yes you can. And please do. After the ladies of The Cut indulged themselves in dizzy speculation about the natural bioengineering and architectural advantages of a man with a pleasantly doughy paunch over his abdominal muscles, picture editor Emily Shornick got to the slightly soft point. 'What's great about dad bod sex,' she avowed, 'is that you know you're gonna have great post-coital snacks. Dad bod definitely has some cheese in the fridge.'

Yes, dad bod does. Four types of cheese, actually.

Now, of course, those of us who are happily endowed with dad bods, thanks to our status as dads with great bods, have no need of all the attention. But it occurs to me that many of you young, whippet-thin Gen Y types might be feeling anxious or even threatened to be surrounded by so many fine examples of paunchy perfection. Fear not. The dad bod can be yours with a minimum of effort. Indeed, the minimum of effort is almost the defining characteristic of the dad bod.

By enrolling in my 12-Week Dad Bod Transformation you can make of yourself the powerful, yet fetchingly broken-down lion in winter that all the ladies are into now.

Please leave your contact details in the comments below for a complimentary copy of my recipe for a three-cheese toasted sandwich and an outline of the 12-Week Dad Bod program, including insider tips on how to do three or four squats at a time, how to safely deadlift a fully stocked esky, and my one weird trick for counting that trip from the couch to the fridge as a serious high-burn abdominal workout.

brisbanetimes.com.au, May 2015

Modern dad

Is there a more shameful moment for the modern dad than a movie which refuses to download? You've set the little ones up on the couch, promised them a feast of *Star Wars* or *Frozen* or the latest instalment of Mr Sylvester Stallone's most excellent *The Expendables*, and now you're staring at the spinning beach ball of death. Not an entertaining beach ball of death such as that used by Mr Jason Statham to brutally kill legions of ne'er-do-wells in *The Expendables Go to Hawaii*. No. The other one, the one that presages an onscreen announcement that your video will be available to watch in 17.5 hours.

Oh woe is the modern dad.

How much easier it must have been for old-fashioned dads in the days when setting up a holiday movie marathon meant flicking on the 13-inch B&W Foster Lindbergh Telebox (with eight shades of grey!) and adjusting the rabbit ear antennae until only two or three ghost images haunted the screen. 'Yay, Dad! You're the best!'

Modern dad doesn't get off that easy. Seriously, I don't think society really appreciates just how much we've had to adapt to this fast-paced go-go world. Old-school dad may have taught you how to drive in the empty supermarket car park on Sunday afternoon, but that place is teeming on Sunday arvo now, and, to be frank, modern dad probably doesn't drive, because the inner city is hell for car owners and you should probably just Uber where you're going anyway.

He may not be able to replace the rubber grip on your cricket bat − those things are really hard to get on, you know − but he is expected to deconflict a five-sector wi-fi zone cobbled together from routers, boosters and AirPlay base stations that are not only incompatible but openly hostile to each other.

Old-school dad may have taken you camping in some national park, but modern dad will camp out for you at EB Games to grab up that midnight pre-order of Black Ops with the bonus zombie map.

And sure, trad dad took a distant interest in your superhero comic book obsession while gently steering you towards reading the newspaper. But modern dad's comic book collection is bigger than yours, and if you clean your room properly he might let you have a look at the Ziploc bag containing all 12 issues of his Marvel Superheroes *Secret Wars* story arc. No, not the 2015 edition, you dag, the original 1984 series! (Modern dad rolls eyes.)

Sydney Morning Herald, November 2015

INSIDE THE SAUSAGE OF POLITICS

Flopping it out

The Opposition leader promised this week that every Australian household would receive a free floppy disk drive and monochrome monitor under an Abbott-led government.

Launching the Coalition's long-awaited response to the government's National Broadband Network program, Mr Abbott denied that providing a floppy drive and monitor without the computing box to plug them into would leave Australian households with a second-best solution.

'Second best is the sort of Labor extravagance that is bankrupting this country,' he said. 'If people want more they can easily spend a few thousand dollars to upgrade to a very fast 386 or even 486 computing box.'

When asked by Leigh Sales what a '386 computing box' was, he admitted he wasn't 'across the brief' but, 'Here's everyone's favourite! The internet's Malcolm Turnbull!'

Mr Turnbull immediately deflected criticism of the lack of a computing box by pointing out that the monochrome monitor was not some old-fashioned TRS-80 green screen, but, rather, a much cooler-looking mandarin-hued model, which was more than adequate for most people's needs.

'WordStar looks smashing on this,' he said.

When asked how much input he'd had into the final policy he smiled and insisted it was all Mr Abbott's work, 'All of it. Nothing to do with me. Make sure you write that down.'

The policy launch, which took place in a futuristic studio setting, and was attended by dozens of the nation's top technology writers, was an accident, sources close to Mr Abbott admitted later.

'It was supposed to be just Tony and Dennis Shanahan,' the spokesman said. 'Dennis can't even read his emails. A secretary types them out for him. We thought he'd be good for us.'

Instead, Mr Abbott had to repeatedly defer to his communications spokesman to handle the demanding technical details of the policy. Mr Turnbull admitted the whole thing was 'really just a bag of dicks', but urged the assembled journalists to take note of how much more impressive he looked than his leader when talking about this stuff.

Mr Abbott, repeatedly trying to plug one of the demo model floppy drives into a power point, said he 'wasn't really a tech head'.

Reaction to the announcement was frothingly positive in the News Limited press, where news that the NBN would not be able to compete with Telstra was hailed as 'excellent' by major shareholder, and noted Sith Lord, Rupert Murdoch.

brisbanetimes.com.au, April 2013

Ho, fellow conservative Australians!

And welcome to this, the foreword to Cory Bernardi's new book. I would like to thank the good senator for inviting me to write a few words, but even more than that, I would like to express my heartfelt appreciation for the very large cheque which made my contribution possible.

Like many of the hundreds of Australians who have rushed online to review *The Conservative Revolution*, I cannot admit to having read it. Unlike them, however, I have very much enjoyed spending the untraceable funds provided by the cabal of multinational mining companies, merchant banks and tax-exempt mega-churches who have endorsed and possibly funded its publication and my latest beachfront property.

While never having had the pleasure of meeting the senator, who must be very careful about his public movements given the insensate rage he seems to inspire in others when he goes about in public, I can assure you that I like the cut of his jib. One only has to gaze into the fathomless depths of his completely black eyes to know that here is a fellow ready to light a fire under the feet of a complacent nation. Or to use a white-hot poker on those unprotected feet, or even a handy pair of pliers, should lighting a fire prove inconvenient because of ill-conceived environmental legislation.

My fellow conservative Australians – and we are all conservative Australians now, thanks to the courageous legislation promoted by Senator Bernardi to strip away the citizenship from anyone who isn't conservative and even from those who'd mask themselves as conservative when we know in fact that they're really about the gay marriage because they secretly want to force everyone to share their secret and shameful and intriguing lusts.

My fellow conservative Australians, we must heed the warning of Cory that the moral relativism of the Left threatens Australia's way of life. Why, if these lentil-eating monsters had their way it would be illegal for a fellow to whip the wretched Chinamen at the steam laundrette for putting too much starch in his dickie, to correct one's bothersome wife with the back of one's hand, or even to launch a simple punitive raid against the natives should they threaten to breach the boundaries at the edge of settlement with their gibbering demands to not be shot or poisoned or run off their so-called ancestral lands.

These are the unflinching standards we must cleave to without flinching, if we are to walk the path 'to a better Australia through a commitment to faith, family, flag, freedom and free enterprise'. The senator has reminded us again and again during his time in parliament that we must 'protect and defend the traditional institutions that have stood the test of time'. Institutions such as restricting the vote to chaps with property holdings of some significance or at the very least a commission in one of the better regiments. Traditions such as White Australia, keeping ladies out of the universities and the working man in his place.

When I think of how our founding governors were able to throw a man in irons, or have him flogged or even hanged for making the sort of trouble we must now routinely endure from Ms Hanson-Young, I cannot help but wonder if we have fallen so far from our first principles that there is no further left to fall.

Cory Bernardi's book is proof that yes, yes there is.

Oh poor fellow, my country, is there anyone brave enough to call our attention away from the hysteria of so-called global warming and onto the existential threat of Malcolm Turnbull? Yes, of course there is. And it's Bernardi! The courage of the man is found in his willingness to challenge the enemy within with the same gimlet-eyed fanaticism he unleashes on the enemy without. Not only does the all-powerful gay lobby with its millions and millions of supporters go weak at the knees with the very idea of a pumped-up and sweating Bernardi having his way with them, but treacherous elements within his own party are likewise cowed.

This well-dressed Turnbull, with his expensive suits and tailor-made liberalism, forever wanting to extend to everyone those freedoms and privileges traditionally reserved for privileged chaps like Bernardi, where does he get off? At the first stop on the road to Greenie Left Hell, that's where. With a quick detour to drop into the wedding reception for a gay marriage between a couple of Muslim fellows.

The senator knows that before he can deal with the gays and Muslims he has to secure himself against the single mothers, and the stepchildren and the divorcees and that Warren Entsch with his suspicious and unmanly earring, but most of all against Turnbull, who, I might add, does not meet the Bernardi Eugenics Gold Standard, hailing as he does from a single-parent home.

There is a reason Turnbull looks ill most every time he has to stand next to the prime minister and explain why a long piece of string and two empty soup cans will outperform the NBN. It's because he is a watermelon. Green on the outside, and red within!

Although it might also be because Mr Abbott once thought himself to have had a child out of wedlock, thus meaning that he too could not measure up to Bernardi's standards.

But who among us can?

Sydney Morning Herald, 2014

Statement by the League of Australians for a Muntstitutional Conarchy on the occasion of the Prime Minister's treasonous plot to raise the Natives above their lowly station

It is with wuthering horror that we note the proposal of Her Majesty's Prime Minister to interfere with Her Majesty's Antipodean Muntstitution such as to effect a recognition of the savages that lately infested this place as if they owned it or something.

We Australians of the Muntstitutional Conarchy League will pull our walking socks all the way up from our proud sandals and thence go to any length to oppose these dangerous shenanigans.

Whilst the dangerous idea of reconciliation with the Natives is a fine, if dangerous, one, it behooves we of the League to warn of the dangers of toying with such ideas lest they lead inevitably into danger. Ne'er do such wild notions creep into the national discourse without much derangement of the national humours, the angryfying of the national temper and the inevitable sheddifying of blood. Not if we have our way they don't.

You will recall that we fulsomely supported the notion of an Apology from the Aboriginal Nation to the lawful owner of Her Majesty's Australian colonies for not really having the place ready for the subjects of her distantly beloved forebear George III. And we of the League, it were, who originally campaigned for the counting of the Natives as an addendum to Her Majesty's census, that policing the boundaries of their Reserves might be more efficiently undertook by the Mounted Regiments.

It is unfair in both the general and particular then to accuse the Muntstitional League of sleeping in our club chairs and tipping the half-full brandy glass of apathy into the tweed-clad lap of indifference on matters concerning the most Wretched Natives. Long have we warned of the very real imperilment they pose to white settlement, having been here so inconveniently, but in a legally unenforceable sense, when then-His Majesty's white men arrived to be about their settling. These, our storied forefathers, did warn His and Her Majesties' Governors of this as they drove the Natives from the waterfront real estate with musket fire, sabre cuts and the pox blankets.

Down through the centuries which made this country the great and united nation it is today, they ensured our greatness by uniting against any remnant black fellows who were in need of running off the best bits of Her Majesty the sainted Victoria's potential grazing lands.

Certainly white settlement was not without its problems, but most of them were killed, and the League believes that had the British not colonised this country and brought with them the concept of law and order, some terrible dago might have, and where would we all be then? Why, we'd be aliens in our own land.

brisbanetimes.com.au, January 2014

From the office of the Prime Minister

To: Australian Archives.
Re: Transcripts, PM's office. November 2013.
(Archival note: present were the Prime Minister,
Foreign Minister, Minister for Stopping Immigration.)

Tony Abbott, Prime Minister: Come in, Jules, Scotty.
You can help me, er, you know, draft the letter to
Bang Bang. Jules, you want to come sit on my lap?
Take some dictation?

Julie Bishop, Foreign Minister: (freezing silence, as vast
as space, as cold as the Vikings' conception of hell)

Abbott: Er, okay, alright. But I am, er, I am the Minister for Women, you know?

Scott Morrison, Minister for Stopping Immigration:
(zombie noises, mostly snarls and sucking gurgles)

Abbott: So, er, I thought, you know, we'd er, send old
Bang Bang a note, and er ... er ... well, I dunno,
can we blame it on Jules?

Bishop: (the sound of frozen air sucked through teeth,
filed to sharp points)

Abbott: Ha! You thought I meant you? No, er, no. I meant the ginger ninja. She's got to earn her, er, she's got to earn her pension somehow now.

Bishop: (hisses) It wasn't her.

Morrison: (snarling. The sound of flesh rending. Bones breaking ... Unintelligible ... Possibly terrified whimpering)

Abbott: Jeez, Scotty. Is that one of those reffo kids? Er, never mind. Just ... er, just chew with your mouth closed, would you? You're getting bits all over the carpet. What was that, Jules? I could er ...

Bishop: It wasn't Gillard. It was Rudd. He was prime minister when we ... or they ... bugged President Yudhoyono.

Abbott: Well, that's good, isn't it? Let's, er, let's go with that. Can you, er, can you take a few notes, Jules? You're, er, you're the Minister for Foreigners, aren't you? Well, the ones we can't lock up anyway. Ha! See what I did there? And Bang Bang's a foreigner. He, er, certainly, he ah, he certainly sounds like one on all the tapes, ah, ASIS send me. Sounds like, er, like he's always got a gob full of, er, nasi bloody goreng.

Morrison: (grunting, unintelligible)

Abbott: So, er, what do we call him, you know, official like but, ah, friendly? What did, er, what did his lady call him? Did ASIS run it, ah, through, er, you know the Google translate thingy. I'm er, you know, I'm not, er, I'm not a techy. I think she called him ... Love Monkey, was that it? Er. Like a nickname or something? Is that what Google said? You reckon we should do that? Dear, er, Love Monkey?

Bishop: (Darth Vader breathing)

Abbott: No? Okay. Er, how about mate, then? Everyone loves being called mate. Obama got a real kick out of it, I think, er, when I called him mate that time. On the, er, phone. He was laughing and everything. Couldn't even stop.

Bishop: (more Darth Vader breathing) Mister President.

Morrison: Braaaaainnzzz.

Abbott: Yeah, okay, we'll do the cross-out thing. Take a note, Jules. 'Dear Mister President'. Then cross it out, and, ah, write in 'Dear Love Monkey'. Like we've, ah, like we've changed our minds. Cos, er, you know, that's the, ah, that's the impression we want to give. Isn't it? That's the impression to give, that we've changed our minds and, ah, we're not gonna spy on the Love Monkeys any more. And, ah, better get ASIS to, ah, check that they believed it. You know, like, ah, can we bug him or something? So, er, we start, off, ah, 'Dear' ... 'Dear Love' ... Oh, look, ah, let's just call him ... let's just call him Bang Bang. Yeah. You getting this, Jules? 'Dear Bang Bang'. Okay. Good start. And we'd better get the, ah, the apologies, out there, you know. Better get them out there? So, ah, let's say, ah, 'Mate, look, ah, I'm, ah, sorry if you're upset about all this. Ah. And I'm really … really … sorry you're, ah, thinking of turning back our juicy beef exports.'

Morrison: Meeeeat. Fleshhhhh …

Abbott: Yeah, Scotty. That's good. Just, just calm down, Scotty. So, Jules, you, ah, you getting this? Let's, ah, let's say, ah, look we'd better, ah, apologise some more. It's like, ah, it's like a culture thing or something, with them, isn't it? It's all about apologising.

Morrison: (snarls, grunts)

Abbott: Oh … I know. I got it. Let's, ah, let's apologise for that, ah, letter, that, ah, you know Scotty sent him, ah … or maybe just for Scotty. Er. You right with that, Scotty? If we chuck in an apology for you?

Morrison: (burps)

Abbott: Great, that's great, mate. So, er, Jules, er, let's say 'We're sorry that Scotty's been, ah, you know, stalking you, Bang Bang', and ah, that er, kid who works for him. What's his name, Marty Alphabet something? Yeah, that's right, 'Marty, er, we're sorry Scotty's been stalking him too, and er, just, er, you know, hanging around down, ah, at the, er, docks and stuff, just, er, you know, stalking people and stuff. We're sorry for that.'

Morrison: (explodes in rage; clanking of chains and manacles)

Abbott: Calm down, Scotty. Let's, ah, Jules, let's, ah … oh I know, let's turn it around, eh. Ah … something like, 'Bang Bang, we're really sorry about', ah, no, no, 'We're so sorry about Scotty crawling in through your, ah, your palace windows and, and you know, ah, your bedroom windows and stuff.' Ah. But, ah … oh, this is good, Jules, get this. Lick the pencil. Yeah, that's good. Make sure it's ah, working. Say 'We're, ah, sorry about Scotty always, er, following him and, ah, jumping out of, er, cupboards and things, but, er, he's, er, just, you know, he's new in the job and, er, if you, ah, think about it, you know, Bang Bang, it ah, goes to prove, ah, it just goes to prove, doesn't it, me old Love Monkey, that, ah, we can't be, ah, you know, listening in or, uhm, reading your, ah, snappy chat, your, uhm, sexy text, ah, any more, because, ah, that's why we've got, ah, Scotty off the leash now. Because we, ah shut down, you know, Labor's great big, ah, new spying scheme. It's gone. All gone.' Brilliant. Yeah! You got that, Jules? Can we, ah, can we get one of the, ah, girls to, er, you know, ah, one of the girls to put it on the good paper? With the roos and emus and things?

Bishop: (a low rumble, like the implosion of a star in a long-dead galaxy)

Abbott: Great! Good, ah, good work, everyone. I reckon we'll, ah, we'll have these love monkeys all over us when I'm done.

brisbanetimes.com.au, November 2013

The ballad of Admiral Morrison

I am the very model of a modern muddled admiral,
I've information nautical, specifical and general,
I know the polls political, and weather patterns
    seasonal,
But have some trouble navigating waters Indonesianal;
I'm very well acquainted too with queries from the
    media,
My answers would be better than the best of
    Wikipedia,
But somewhere twixt my press release and stories so
    sensational,
Everything gets covered up with matters operational.
I'm very good at shifting blame and demonising boat
    people,
I know a dozen different ways of bamboozilising most
    sheeple,
In short, in matters nautical but not so navigational,
I am the very model of a modern muddled admiral.
I know our mythic history, the yellow peril and the
    policy,

Of keeping all the nice things for the white folk as a
    courtesy,
To white folk who are just a little frightened of the
    heresy,
Of sharing all their nice things instead of guarding
    them so jealously.
I can tell a queue jumper from foreigners legitimate,
But have a little trouble with my compass and the
    intimate
Way those Indonesianals pack a fellow into it
When they pack a fellow into a facility correctional
Just because a fellow has no facility directional!
That I should be imprisoned now seems a damned
    effrontery,
Worse than this bowl of grasshoppers the guard just
    put in front of me,
In short, in matters nautical and consequence ironical
I am the very model of a modern muddled admiral.

brisbanetimes.com.au, January 2014

From Scott Morrison
Minister for Stopping Immigration

To the President of Indonesia

Listen, you

I've had just about enough of this. In case you hadn't noticed, we had an election a while ago and I won and you didn't, so I'd suggest you pull your socks up, or whatever you people wear instead of civilised shoes and socks, and get a double swift hurry along taking back all those ghastly little brown people you let escape into our backyard.

And don't think I didn't notice the way you dressed one of them up like a bloody cricketer the other day. Oh yes, big laughs all around the bloody Presidential Palace, I'm sure. But I don't suppose you bothered to stop and think about the family of the poor Aussie cricketer who's now out of a job because your blasted queue-jumper jumped the bloody queue right into the Test squad for Brisbane.

You tell that cheeky bloody foreign minister of yours I've got his number. Literally. ASIS gave it to me along with his credit card details, and if we have any more pranks or dusky new opening batsmen sent our way, 'Party' Marty Natawhatshisname will be getting more than one of Julie Bishop's liver-frying stares. He can expect a large truckload of VHS tapes featuring the finest work of Japan's foremost tentacle porn directors to arrive at the Foreign Ministry to make a very bloody public delivery in his name on the receipt of his signature. Which I also have.

I'm sorry things have come to this, but, Jesus, you people are frustrating to deal with. You won't do as you're told. You won't do what I promised. It's as if you weren't even paying attention When I Won The Election.

Let me repeat that. I won, and you didn't, and I am your government now.

I don't even know why this is a problem for you. Believe me when I say we know everything going on inside your so-called country, and I know for a fact that Indonesia is full to pussy's bow with little brown people. So it's not like you'd even notice a couple more. You could put them on one of your unpopular islands with the gila monsters and volcanoes. We'll even pay you, or a nominated account in the tax haven of your choice, to take them there. It could be a win all round if some of our journos, who've given you as much grief as me, tried to follow them up there and met with an accident.

Unpredictable beast, your gila monster. As happy to snack on Bridie Jabour as dodo eggs, I'm told.

So come on now, Bang Bang, let's be reasonable. We can hardly move on the M4 of an afternoon, it's so jammed up with your bloody fishing boats full of Afghan cricketers, and we've burned so many of the bloody things down to their rotting keels that you must surely be feeling the pinch at the local fish-'n'-chip shop by now.

What do you say? One last chance to help out a mate?

No need to bother hitting reply. ASIS can tell me what you say.

Yours

Scott

Sydney Morning Herald, November 2013

Spy vs spy

I am shocked, shocked I tell you, to discover that our nefarious spy agencies have been spying on some guys. Some of these guys are likewise understandably and volubly shocked and outraged to discover they have been spied upon by our spies. The second-most shocked and outraged of all are all the guys who've been spying on our spies while our spies were spying on their guys. But the most shocked of everyone who has been shocked and appalled by all of these shenanigans is the delightfully naive Greens leader Christine Milne.

'We're up to our neck in it!' she gasped last week, when learning, apparently for the first time, that (1) spies were a thing, (2) we had a heap o' them, and (3) they were spying on people!

(Next week, Senator Milne discovers that the army is not just a branch of the rural fire service. Pratfalls and hilarity, guaranteed. 'They do what? Omigod! Who gave them all those guns?')

This week, however, it's about the other guy who's

shocked, shocked, he'll tell you, that Australian spies have been spying on his guys. Indonesian foreign minister and serial prankster Marty Natalegawa hasn't had this much fun with stony-faced Australian counterpart Julie Bishop since all those private notes of their closed-door meeting suddenly flew out the wide open door of his hotel suite and into the hands of the waiting media, where they suddenly weren't very private any more.

While Senator Milne has amused everyone with her delightful ingenue act – what did she imagine all those line items for 'cloaks and daggers' in the ASIS budget were actually buying? – it's the ANU graduate Marty who's bringing the real lulz to this spy scandal. Marty Natalegawa, who, as Indonesian foreign minister, regularly pores over the reports from Badan Intelijen Negara (BIN), the Indonesian State Intelligence Agency, and Lembaga Sandi Negara or LEMSANEG, the Indonesian equivalents of ASIS and the Defence Signals Directorate respectively.

On first blush, BIN in particular might seem to be the sort of spy agency that Senator Milne would approve of, if Senator Milne ever approved of such things, which she doesn't, so don't even go there. BIN's jaunty website, out there for all the world to see, features a story on its home page about 'The Women of BIN' attending a seminar on food safety, which is very important because unsafe food is not safe. So good on BIN for making sure the lady spies have that covered.

(And good on them, too, for answering questions on the site about whether they kidnapped prominent Indonesian academic and chairman of the Democrat Party Professor Subur Budhisantoso. Long answer short? 'We didn't do it nobody saw us you can't prove anything. What? The professor? Why, he's … he's right over there … off in the jungle … yes, that shadow over there … that's him. No, don't get any closer! Look out! There are tigers!')

But the State Intelligence Agency has gathered a little more responsibility to itself than totally not kidnapping any more professors and making sure the benches are wiped down in the national tuckshop. BIN coordinates the collection activities and operations of all Indonesia's intelligence agencies, and runs its own operations against targets both foreign and domestic, including Australian agencies, companies and individuals. Marty Natalegawa has well earned his pay cheque this week pushing back against the efforts of the US and Australian agencies much more effectively than the counterintelligence sections of BIN and LEMSANEG have ever done.

It still leaves all those other agencies though, doesn't it? Not the cowboy US and Australian outfits, but the Chinese, Japanese, Korean, Malaysian, Singaporean and, what the hell, even Papuan ones.

Yes, Papua New Guinea has big-boy pants and its very own spy agency too: the National Intelligence Organization, which conducts covert foreign operations on the direct say so of the prime minister.

Sure, that mostly means using a fake ID in a Port Moresby internet cafe to cyber-stalk Marty Natalegawa's Facebook timeline, but A for Effort, Papua New Guinea. It's just super to have you along. And really, you shouldn't be embarrassed that the NIO is just two blokes with an old Pentium box and a green screen monitor in a shed out the back of Parliament House. It's a crowded, hyper-competitive field, international espionage, and while the acronym gang of ASIS and DSD and the NSA and CIA hog all the limelight, you can be sure they don't get everything their way.

There's those pesky parliamentary and congressional oversight thingies to contend with, and the press of course, and now all the tech giants like Apple and Google cutting up rough. Not like in Korea, where the National Intelligence Service works hand in glove – or fist in chain mail – with the country's giant techno-industrial combines such as Samsung and LG, placing agents inside private corporations as part of its mission of 'strengthening economic security'. Or like China, which the running dogs of the Federation of

American Scientists estimate has field agents of the Ministry of State Security scattered across 50 countries and in more than 170 cities.

While China has been as publicly shocked, yes shocked, and upset as Indonesia by the 'revelation' of the Five Eyes, or 'Echelon' spy network (the anglophone democracies, basically), the existence of the US-led operation has long been detailed on Greg Hunt's favourite intelligence resource, Wikipedia. Perhaps, to be fair, however, the Chinese spies didn't have time to look up the page because they were too busy running their vast human intelligence network stealing business and technology secrets from all over the globe.

In the end, spies gonna spy. It's what they've always done and always will. Every country will lean on its competitive advantages in the field. For China that means vast legions of foot soldiers. For the US and other Echelon nations, it means preferencing their technological superiority.

For Indonesia, at the moment, it means using the shadow puppet theatre of hurt pride and umbrage to force its opponents to back off.

And for New Guinea, it's always time to do a little Facebook stalking.

Sydney Morning Herald, November 2013

Minutes of an intelligence briefing

The Oval Office
Subject: UKRAINE/RUSSIA
Present:
POTUS
General Biff McBrisket (Head of NSA)
Admiral 'Big' Dick 'Nautical' Miles USN Ret'd (Head of CIA)
Sir Talbot Duckenweave (Head of UK SIS)
Meeting commenced with the President thanking Sir Talbot for making the effort to fly to Washington to personally brief him on the findings of British Intelligence. POTUS asked if Duckenweave would like a cup of coffee, but Sir Talbot said he preferred tea, with a crumpet if at all possible. Crumpets were secured. Tea was served. Tea was rejected on the basis of being a dangly bag, not a proper pot thereof.

Admiral Miles said a rude word. General McBrisket had to be asked to put down his iPad.

POTUS asked who had the most up-to-date intel on the situation.

McBrisket said that NSA was all over it.

POTUS gave him permission to turn on his iPad again.

Head of NSA McBrisket reported that Angela Merkel was secretly backing Latvia, to which POTUS responded he hadn't realised Latvia had been drawn into the confrontation between Moscow and Kiev. Head of NSA rolled his eyes and went 'Pfft' as if POTUS didn't even know what he was talking about, because Latvia was totally going to take out *Eurovision* this year and although Merkel had to publicly support the German contestants, XWORD FILTER ECHELON intercepts of her private cell phone had caught her telling Mister Merkel that she thought Latvia …

Head of NSA trailed off when he looked up from his iPad and saw the President's face.

POTUS indicated, forcefully, that he was not interested in Chancellor Merkel's wagers on the *Eurovision Song Contest* and was instead seeking actionable intelligence he might use to respond to the current crisis.

'You might have noticed the crisis, General; it's been on all the news channels,' said the President.

Sir Talbot Duckenweave put down his crumpet and, after removing the butter from his fingers by using it to twirl the ends of his handlebar moustache, declared that the President was quite right. McBrisket had completely ignored the crisis which was straining the resources of Her Majesty's Secret Intelligence Service to its limit.

POTUS asked that Sir Talbot elaborate.

'Well, they're all starkers, of course. All of them. It's all anyone at HQ can talk about. One hardly knows where to look.'

POTUS responded that he wasn't sure what the Head of SIS meant.

POTUS asked, 'Did you mean the Russians are "stark raving mad"? Is that the English term?'

Sir Talbot responded that, no, his service was in an absolute tizz because, of the millions of hours of video chat they'd intercepted and analysed so far, most of the take consisted of subjects without pants waving their wobbly bits at the camera.

'You've got footage of Putin's wobbly bits?' POTUS demanded to know.

'Who?' Sir Talbot asked. 'Oh, him? No.' Head of SIS explained that the Secret Service did not have to break in on any encrypted traffic to see Mr Putin's wobbly bits. 'He's forever flopping them in public.'

No, explained Sir Talbot. SIS had effected a major intelligence-gathering coup by hacking open Yahoo's video chat service and siphoning off the entire archive which, as he'd just explained, had turned out to mostly consist of people flashing each other their rude bits.

It was more than his poor analysts could stand. He explained that, 'Most of these people on the internet have let themselves go. They are not easy to look at, Mr President.'

POTUS looked at Sir Talbot for quite a long time, saying nothing.

'Admiral Miles?' he sighed at last, turning to Head of CIA. 'Do you have anything for me?'

'Do I ever!' Miles cried out.

POTUS held up one hand and asked Head of CIA if he had anything on the Russian military intervention in Ukraine. Head of Central Intelligence demurred, saying, no, not exactly. But he did have comprehensive coverage of attempts by a Mister Dermott Terwilliger of Beaver's Lick, Arkansas, to secure himself a second Russian bride on the internet because the first one was 'all wore out'.

POTUS asked in quite a cold voice what that had to do with the situation in the Ukraine. Head of CIA pointed out that a lot of people, like Mister Putin for example, often mistook Ukraine for being part of Russia and so this Terwilliger character would bear much closer examination.

Sir Talbot opined that if it was the same Terwilliger he'd seen on Yahoo video chat he could assure everyone that the fellow in question actually didn't bear looking at very closely indeed.

POTUS brought the meeting to a close with the sound of his quiet weeping.

Sydney Morning Herald, March 2014

The new reality

Declaring reality to be incompatible with legitimate Russian interests, President Vladimir Putin has committed more forces to the war in Syria while telling US counterpart Barack Obama to 'move along now, is nothing to see here'. Moscow has ignored warnings from NATO and Washington that it is making things worse, with the Kremlin declaring it had learned the lessons from Afghanistan and that this time they would not waste ten years denying reality.

'Russian forces have begun total war on reality already,' declared Defence Minister Oleg Smersh.

The initial Russian assault opened with repeated denials that a widely observed military build-up in the Syrian port city of Latakia was even a real thing. Unmoved by pictures of Russian fighter bombers and helicopter gunships suddenly appearing without explanation at the city's airport, Minister Smersh at first retorted that it is simply impossible for such things to happen.

'Whoever heard of such big heavy things appearing anywhere with no possible way to explain how they got there?' he asked. 'Do you know how much one of those gunships weighs? They are very heavy, especially when full of bullets and exploding bombs. Did all these things somehow magically fly to Syria? Please, have some dignity.'

When the same fighter bombers made unauthorised incursions into Turkish airspace, President Putin declared himself implacably opposed to admitting anything of the sort.

'Pfft! Turkish airspace? What even is that?' he asked the UN General Assembly last week. 'Can you see this so-called airspace? Can you touch it? No. It is invisible. So is not even real thing then.'

Western military analysts responded with a series of face-palms and head-desks, having no other answer to the Kremlin's new strategy of 'hybrid war'.

First used in the annexation of the Crimea, hybrid war is a sophisticated meshing of doctrine, strategy and tactics to create the impression that invading a neighbouring state was all the idea of two or three drunken military tourists and should not be taken seriously by anybody, especially those countries now full of thousands of Russian tourists and heavy armoured divisions.

The Kremlin's newest war-fighting strategy was perfected in the war with Ukraine, when Putin first declared there was no war, then that there was no Ukraine, and finally that he didn't do it, nobody saw him do it, you can't prove anything. The Syrian government, meanwhile, welcomed the arrival of thousands of Russian tourists with their own air and artillery support.

Facing demands from the Senate Armed Services Committee to explain what America was doing to counter Russia's lead in reality denial, the chairman of the Joint Chiefs of Staff General Biff McBeefburger insisted the US remained an implacable foe of reality and cited the hundreds of millions of dollars which had already been spent training three or four guys to be Syria's moderate opposition forces.

'Those three or four guys represent everything we've tried and failed to achieve in Syria. Don't tell me we're not the world's best at keeping our heads in our asses,' said McBeefburger, arguing that while the Russians had always relied on the sheer bulk of their delusions, America retained a significant advantage in the sophistication of its denials of reality.

'Not everyone can tick a box in the Pentagon and make a Médecins Sans Frontières hospital blow up on the other side of the world,' said McBeefburger. 'But we can, and we did, and nobody can take away our confused and furious denials of what actually happened.'

Sydney Morning Herald, October 2015

Let Turnbull be Turnbull

There has never been a more exciting time to write a column about the year ahead in politics, unless it was last year, or the one before that. Hopefully not. If 2016 delivers anything, fingers crossed, it's a refreshing return to the good old days when the only people who got to roll an incumbent PM were the great big sunburned masses of this great big sunburned continent. As much fun as it was following the slow-motion train wreck of Tony Abbott's prime ministership, after the slow-motion train wreck of Julia Gillard's prime ministership and Kevin Rudd's before (and after) hers, it's probably time to get back into our sensible pants and start thinking about government as something more than a rival reality show stealing ratings from the Kardashian Empire.

Thus, while we of the Satirists Union endorse the former PM Abbott's fond imagining of himself as Menzies in exile and Churchill in exile and look forward almost as much as he does to his inevitable return from exile, the country as a whole, and the government in particular, could really do with a break. Perhaps actual exile to the Vatican as ambassador to George Pell might appeal to the one-time Jesuit and open up the prospect of Malcolm Turnbull finally peeling off the lifelike rubber mask of Abbott he's been forced to wear since taking over, lest he frighten poor Eric Abetz into some crazy-US-rancher-style siege.

'Let Turnbull be Turnbull' will be our watchword this year. The internet's favourite merchant banker has ever so many spiffing ideas for turning John Howard's share-owning democracy into a start-up nation of rock stars, ninjas and gurus doing moonshots, growth hacking and disrupterthons, that it could be almost as entertaining as watching his predecessor have his way with a raw onion. If only the Opposition would get out of the way. No, not that Opposition. The other one, the one that sits behind him and plots the return of the Onion King.

As for Her Majesty's loyal Opposition, what might we expect of them? In the olden days of not so long ago, Bill Shorten would have his back to the wall now, just in case one of his loyal troops tried sticking something sharp and hurty in there. He's protected by changes to the way Labor now choose their fall guys, and by nobody else really wanting the worst job in politics. He could spend the year coming up with new policies, but we in the media will just ignore all his press releases and complain about him not coming up with any new policies.

Assuming the punters do care about such things, and they're not all quietly drooling into their bibs during the ad breaks for *I'm a Celebrity … Get Me Out of Here!* what would they like to see?

A small, ugly minority would probably thrill to a pogrom or two, but they're unlikely to be satisfied with Turnbull's quietly maintaining the machinery of refugee persecution without the riotous theatre of cruelty in its public presentation. Opponents of off-shore processing – or, to be more accurate, lack of processing – will likewise be disappointed when their calls for reform come to nothing. Given the crisis in Europe, Australia is unlikely to change its settings. Most people will probably be happy not to think about any of it.

As the budget approaches they will probably start thinking about what's in it for them, for good or ill, and perhaps this will be the year that the average punter finally rebels at the rather grotesque display of giant corporations paying absurdly small amounts of tax, while corporate lobbyists demand 'tax reform' – presumably so that they might legally pay none at all, without having to go to the tiresome trouble of hiding their profits in an Irish post office box. Scott Morri-son, who spent his early days as treasurer insisting the country had a spending problem, not a revenue problem, has been very quiet of late. It could be that as he has tried to balance the books, he too has come to resent the billions of dollars in company profits which mysteriously never turn into company taxes.

Still, it's a lot harder taking money off Rupert Murdoch than it is mugging a simple pensioner of similar vintage.

The various money pits into which Morrison has to shovel ever-diminishing piles of cash – health, welfare and education being the largest – will all be looking for special treatment. Health, a responsibility split with the states, is likely hostage to reform of the GST. Education reforms await new minister Simon Birmingham pulling a giant rabbit out of a hat, so that the giant rabbit can pull billions of dollars out of its delightfully fluffy arse, to make something happen.

Defence will move from the meaningless excitement of tiny wars far away to the real challenge of block obsolescence as the platforms bought during the Beazley era approach the end of their operational lives. Submarines and jet fighters are the big-ticket items, and both replacement programs are fraught. Voters don't think much on these issues, until somebody buggers them up, at which point everyone becomes an armchair expert in strategy and military procurement; 2016 feels like one of those years.

It is also, of course, the year of the US presidential

election, and as hard as we are on our elected representatives, it's instructive sometimes to look at the clown circus of American politics to remember that we don't have it too bad.

The New Daily, February 2016

There is no such thing as $22 avocado toast

But maybe there should be. Ridonculous demographer Humbert Blowave may simply have been meeting his clickbait KPIs when he set the dumpster on fire over the weekend, claiming that kids these days should be driving trucks for their country and negatively gearing their second McMansion instead of gallivanting about the boulevards combing truffled avo toast from their hipster beards – but his was the hot take we desperately needed.

Not because he was right – he was the exact opposite of right – but because our long national nightmare is over at last. Finally, we can have the angry, undignified discussion we should have had about smashed avocado a long time ago.

I put it to you, my friends, that the day is come for us to tip the old, cold bowl of spaghetti bolognese off its pedestal as our national dish and replace it with – yay! – smashed avocado toast.

Spagbol has had its run, but avocado toast has been a victim of prejudice so entrenched in our system that it is sparking revolt across the West in general, and most specifically here in this column where I'm talking about it.

What am I talking about? you ask, the way you always do.

Avocado toast and bigotry, that's what. For although none dare call it bigotry, this is the endgame of Humbert Blowave and his ilk.

Think about it.

How can spaghetti bolognese remain our national dish when it has proven itself wholly unsuitable as a breakfast option? I will concede, under duress, that it will do for lunch, but only after steeping overnight at the back of the fridge in the form of conveniently microwavable leftovers.

No, spagbol is an entirely reasonable dinner, but not a national dish.

Only smashed avocado, available on toast at all three main meal times, and as a tasty snack at all the other hours in between, has the versatility to be on our coat of arms, and the sustainable price-to-earnings ratios that will keep generations of avocado miners down in the giant open-cut avo pits of far north Queensland for generations to come.

They are the ones I worry about if Blowave should ever have his actual way. He may not care about the livelihoods of those hard-working men and women who risk everything to dig our precious green golden nuggets of goodness from trees deep beneath the earth, but all right-thinking Australians do. And if a $22 plate of avo toast is the price we pay for our precious freedoms then that is a price I am willing to pay, as long as there's some fried haloumi too.

brisbanetimes.com.au, October 2017

Exciting marketing opportunity

In modern marketing there is no exciting customer service opportunity quite as exciting as the opportunity to charge mug punters more for less. Gouging ever more money for diminishing services and shabbier products is what the new economy is all about. The packet of potato chips with more air than chip is 'Now lighter and healthier!' Four-dollar interns crowd out those insanely expensive teenaged casuals. And letting rich people pay for the right to stampede over the top of poor people at the airport can only result in greater numbers of rich people flying in to enjoy themselves doing just that.

Tucked away in the budget fine print was an innovation which would allow 'premium' airline passengers to skip the less than premium experience of having to line up with the lower orders at Customs and Immigration. After all, it's hardly fair. Having paid such a steep price for those business and first-class tickets it be must a dreadful thing having to actually mix with the riffraff while waiting to escape the terrible crush at the baggage carousel, or the bleary-eyed and undeniably smelly line for passport and visa stamps. Why, it's almost as though one were expected to rub elbows with them – dry, scabbed, scaly elbows off which the most hideous flakes of inflamed and crusty poorperson skin might peel at any moment. Heaven forfend!

The Turnbull government, which is possessed of the smoothest, most exquisitely moisturised elbows, proposes to charge airport operators a fee for the premium fast-lane service, but will not disclose how much revenue they expect to make, citing commercial confidentiality. In such circumstances it is best to let Withnail and I be your guide. Such things are virtually free to those who can afford them, and very expensive to those who can't.

Where might this end, one wonders.

One very obvious place suggests itself. As tedious and unpleasant as an hour spent in the line at Customs might be, it is as nothing compared to the many, many, many hours you can spend lined up at Centrelink. Do not for a moment imagine that the downtrodden and penurious hangers-on at the old welfare shop have neither the readies nor the inclination to pay up. If tabloid TV and tabloid tabloids have taught us nothing, and they totally haven't, it's that the country is overrun by dole-bludging millionaires and cashed-up welfare cheats. Surely they could be touched up for a contribution to the consolidated revenue they're so enthusiastically unsolidating with their rapacious call on the Commonwealth? Perhaps something like a gold class at the movies would tempt them to pay a little back. I imagine a small but significant charge, the exact sum to be commercial-in-confidence naturally, to enjoy a nice sit-down in a Centrelink-branded Smoky Dawson recliner-rocker with cable and/or streaming TV and an adult beverage. The comprehensiveness of the channel selection and the alcohol content of said beverage would of course be determined on a user pays basis.

Something similar might work well in public hospitals, with wealthier patients able to jump the queue, choose their physician and nominate all sorts of expensive elective procedures simply by paying for them. After all, it's a system that's worked very well in private health care for many years. Why have we not trialled it in the public system? So too with public schools, which are reportedly quite terrible. If people were willing to pay for the ovals and blazers and brutal hazing rituals, there's no reason Rooty Hill High could not compete directly with Melbourne Grammar. They just have to be free to charge lots and lots of money.

Once you free yourself from the idea of equity and the public good – indeed, once you recognise that the best public good is the one you buy to shut out the other guy – there is very little this new model of public policy could not improve. I for one look forward to buying my own SAS regiment to keep the riffraff from bothering me as I enjoy a bit of Netflix and Grange while civilisation as we once understood it is sold off to the highest bidder.

The New Daily, May 2016

I read Senator Malcolm Roberts's scorching indictment of the CSIRO's criminal conspiracy to ruin us all so you wouldn't have to

Roberts's report needs only a little more Comic Sans and Pepe the Frog to make it a classic of the genre. It cunningly borrows the language of science to lure science into a sketchy back alley so Pepe can jump out with an axe handle and give that stupid science the vicious beatdown it's been asking for.

Ha! Peer review that, science.

'There is no justification for saying that human carbon dioxide output determines carbon dioxide levels in the air,' the Roberts report declares.

Carbon dioxide levels are instead a natural phenomenon, which anybody who's done the requisite reading on the dark web knows is a false flag operation to cover the chemtrails of the United Nations black helicopters, as they crisscross the flat earth (more on this in Volume 2!) seeking out innocent victims for their alien butt-probe experiments.

Of course, you would already know this if you haunted the right online discussion boards and if you had not been duped by a corrupt mass media in league with the cute cuddly animal lobby and the powerful interests behind baby dolphins.

Oh, what's that?

You doubt the pernicious influence of dolphins? Then riddle me this: why does Australia, with the world's largest fishing zone, import three-quarters of the seafood we eat? It's not just because of those dodgy little prawns in the fried rice we were forced to put in our meat pies when Malcolm Fraser threw open the gates to his refugee mates so that somebody would watch his failing SBS network that he owned.

Ask yourself, as I did while reading Senator Roberts's report and adjusting the wire coathanger I use as an alpha-wave filter, could it be because we have to compete with dolphins?

Why, yes! Yes it could.

Allow me to adjust the alpha waves and consider the empirical evidence in a way the CSIRO never does. Dolphins eat fish fingers and love them so much they would keep all of our fish fingers for themselves if they could.

Our seas are teeming with fish fingers, but even though we are sovereign citizens we have to get our fish fingers from the freezer aisle at Woolies.

This is important, because as the senator reminds us in this report, 'In the mid-1970s we were warned of imminent, catastrophic irreversible damage due to humans causing global freezing.'

But the freezing never happened.

And who profited from that, I ask you?

The dolphins, of course.

It's always the dolphins.

If you would just read Senator Roberts's report you would understand this and all the other things too.

brisbanetimes.com.au, November 2016

Election wrap

It's always tempting to think our elections blow chunks. Corrosive self-doubt and the national cringe reflex were especially strong this year when we had to compete with Brexit and the looming US ballot. You don't have a hope against class acts like The Donald and Farage. Satan's own giant sentient turnip in a hairpiece? A dangerous idiot sewn together from the facial expressions of the Monty Python cast doing a theatre-sports bit on reacting to their first sniff of bottled Belgian farts? No, not even Barnaby Joyce can compete with that.

A US election gone bad after the shock of Britain's Brexit vote could conceivably usher in the end of the actual world. The best our local campaigners could hope for was a hashtag that might trend for a couple of hours, powered by the nation's collective drollery. #FakeTradie was that hashtag.

It was almost as though former PM Toned Abs' love of hi-vis and hard hats was so intense it distorted reality for anybody who wandered too close, as the current PM, Chauncy Turncoat, was obliged to when he forcefully inserted that rather large butcher's knife between Abs' shoulder blades. Other than a temporary fit of madness, how else to explain spending all those ill-gotten campaign funds on a TV ad that did not so much inspire voters to contemplate the Gordian knot of housing and tax policy as it encouraged them to lay in a supply of adult diapers lest they ruin another pair of underpants in a totally unexpected moment of boisterous merriment?

For a short while, in the dying moments of the campaign, it seemed as though Kelly O'Dwyer's #FakeFamily might unseat #FakeTradie from his King-of-Comedy throne. In a rookie move, however, she distracted attention from her campaign flyer featuring nearly lifelike mannequins posed in an almost natural family scene by going to war with Twitter. Not with the many, many Twitter users who would have loved nothing more than a cage match with the government minister whose only previous claim to fame was a disastrous *Q&A* fight with unemployed truck driver Duncan Storrar. No. She went to war with for reals Twitter, the social media giant, when her staff may just possibly, perhaps, have faked a copyright claim to shut down a small parody account that had been embarrassing her in front of its 200 pornbot followers. It's unlikely any of those hot internet MILFs cared whether Kelly O'Dwyer was actually Sophie Mirabella in a convincing mask, but thanks to the Streisand Effect the small parody account is now significantly bigger.

The real Mirabella famously made an unusually frank contribution to honesty in public life when she told a live TV audience that the punters of Wangaratta had lost ten million bucks in hospital funding, which the government trousered after she was dumped by ingrate voters in 2013. Perhaps if the ALP had been as forthcoming about their costings in the last week they might have held onto their small lead in the polls.

'Look, yes, these numbers are pure arse with frostings of arse, but speaking of arse, at least we're not obsessed by it like Cory Bernardi. Vote for us. We're not Cory.'

Whether or not the post-Abs government was actually Cory was probably the through line of the whole election. Other than that expensive coffee table which had to be replaced after it was mysteriously destroyed during the deposed PM's impromptu goodbye toga party, not much else changed, did it? For a couple of weeks there we lived through the most exciting time to be an Australian, ever, until the sneaking suspicion snuck up on everyone who'd put their faith in PM Turncoat that this was just the same old same old but with an appreciably better wardrobe and less chance of onion breath. Opposition leader Bert Short-One offered a promise of change, but that change was mostly about One Weird Trick You Won't Believe Can Help Lose So Much Belly Fat!

Continuity with Change. The PM pinched the slogan from TV's *Veep*, but after this timid, small target campaign by both sides, punters heading into the ballot box could be forgiven for assuming the more things change, the more they will totally stay the same.

It seems many Brexit voters are already wishing they had.

cheeseburgergothic.com, July 2016

I can haz *kompromat?*

Rumours of face-fucking a dead pig's head didn't drive conservative British PM David Cameron from high office, and rumours about paying Russian hookers to wet the bed are no more likely to bring down aggravated Cheezel demon Donald Trump.

You live in a new reality now.

Even if some half-cut Russian spook decided to trouser one or both of the competing bounties being offered for video evidence of confronting orange perversity – a million bucks from *Penthouse* and another million from pornographer emeritus at *Hustler*, Larry Flynt – what harm could it do. Seriously? That would be like asking a gigantic puckered monkey sphincter to care about an obscure rhetorical exchange between classical Greek philosophers. The sphincter just wants what it wants.

Some failed British spy says Trump used prostitutes? Sad!

Dude, any prostitutes woulda been better paid than the subcontractors he's got suing him and, bonus points, they'd have been consenting adults – unlike the dozen or so women who allege Trump sexually assaulted them.

Assuming any sex tape did not inconvenience the President-elect by revealing him to be a grotesque human skin-suit pulled over the ambulatory life-support chassis for a comically small but sentient talking peehole, he's cool. Modern celebrity is not discommoded by scandal; it is enabled and embiggened. Nothing in Trump's rise to power suggests otherwise. The opposite in fact.

At his presser this week, at which he was finally supposed to jelly wrestle the Lovecraftian horror show of his ethical and business conflicts, he instead put on an even better show. Leaping out of the octagon, and into the audience of journalists, he pounded on them with the seething calamari basket of bulging muscular tentacles that normally stay tightly wrapped under his off-the-rack Brioni suits.

As the *New Yorker*'s Amy Davidson reported, just before a jumbo Trumpian sucker nodule closed over her head and silenced her forever:

> Trump looked angry, in a way that, as anger sometimes does, left him more rhetorically focussed. The rambling defensiveness that criticisms often provoke in him was not so

visible. His grandiosity, his resentments, and, at moments, his crudity were all on full display, but not in a way that is likely to alienate his supporters.

Rather than wallowing in a shame bath of fart bubbles and ethical failure after getting doxxed by BuzzFeed, he won the day by teabagging the most embarrassing but least consequential 'revelation' in the data dump – the golden shower Moscow moment. It's an air-quotes revelation because, just like Hillary Clinton's profitable foray into human trafficking and pizza delivery, it remains what journalists refer to technically as 'insane unproven bullshit'.

But in the new reality, it's bullshit that works strangely well. For Trump.

As beguiling as it is to contemplate the spectre of Baron von Clownstick ruining an exquisite set of hotel bedsheets, it is, to quote Admiral Ackbar, a trap. Fuming like a pantsless granddad hot on the trail of his stolen TV dinner, the soon-to-be leader of the free world was allowed to Godwin his own press conference after BuzzFeed published those reports by former British spy Christopher Steele. It was a smear tactic worthy of the Nazis, said Trump.

Steele, now waiting to find out which Russian intelligence service assassinates him first, was hired to dig up 'opposition research' on Trump, specifically focusing on his connections to Moscow. Steele kept at his research even during the brief periods he did not have a paying client. He had become convinced the Russians had a glove puppet candidate in Trump – so convinced he eventually turned his research over to British and US intelligence.

It is of course a delicious irony that Trump's rumoured Moscow sex tapes might have no more basis in reality than Barack Obama's rumoured Kenyan birth certificate, but while the interwebz fell on the BuzzFeed reveal like a labrador on a T-bone, it was not the meat of Steele's investigation. Most of his work turned on a years-long effort by Russian intelligence to cultivate Trump – not because Vladimir Putin had decided he'd like to carve a grotesquely bloated likeness of his own image into a sticky, man-sized lump of boneless ham, just to see whether it could beat Marco Rubio in a cage fight (spoiler: it could), but rather because Trump might be a useful source of gossip on Putin's frenemies and rivals among the Russian oligarch class.

To the permanently appalled he is a vulgarian face-anus in a fright wig, but the billionaire real-estate mogul also mixed with persons of interest to the Russian state. Ignore the golden showers, and Steele has a much more interesting story to tell about the development of Trump as a potential source and asset, and as a foil for Putin against the hated Hillary Clinton. As with any useful idiot, it was not necessary that Trump be aware of his role. The hairpiece does not need to understand its motivation.

Steele concluded, however, that as the election season unrolled, the Trump campaign, if not the candidate, did actively and consciously engage with Putin's security apparatus. It was not always a smooth exchange. At various times his sources reported serious divisions within the Kremlin over fears that email hacking operations were spiralling out of control. Two sources told Steele that the head of the presidential administration, Sergei Ivanov, had fallen out with Putin's spokesman, Dmitry Peskov, over the escalating blowback. For sure, the FSB and GRU could make Clinton's emails appear on the front page of the *New York Times*, but their US counterparts could make all of the euros disappear from your Swiss bank account.

Nobody wants that, comrade.

How much of what Steele reported is true?

Who knows? He was not carrying out a real-time surveillance operation, but rather trying to piece together movement and intent from second- and third-hand sources, well after the fact and at a far remove. As a former spy who operated in Russia, he could not return there. As the former lead analyst on the

Russian desk for the British secret service, he also knew to be wary of Russian disinformation. If Putin's original intent was simply to bungle-fuck Western liberal democracy, he would run dark against Trump as well as Clinton. In that case, Steele's dossier would be full of dezinformatsiya.

The only way to know would be to unleash the CIA and NSA on the case.

The professionals have about a week and a half left before they start taking orders from all of the glistening monkey boners the Trump transition team is currently sliding through the confirmation process.

aliensideboob.com, January 2017

Why I voted for Cthulhu

Sure, I laughed off Cthulhu like everyone else. I'll admit that at first, compared with the other candidates, He looked like a joke. They all presented really well in those TV debates with their fancy store-bought suits and ties. He sort of shambled onstage draped in the glistening skin of his enemies and all their children. But once I stopped laughing at Him and started listening, and I mean really listening, to his guttural snarls and burps, He started to win me over. I felt like once you got past the pouchy crocodile eyes, the bluster and the unpredictable geysers of digestive acid you could just tell He really was interested in you.

It was the way He looked at you. With a sort of hunger.

None of the other candidates gave me that feeling. They wanted my vote.

Cthulhu wanted me.

I understand He's not a perfect man by any means. I mean, let's face it, He's not a man at all. More of a smoking blob of evil dragon jizz with tentacles

and teeth, but in a vaguely human form. He kind of
reminds me of my ex-husband like that. I think deep
down, like Gary, He's basically good. You just have to
look past the bad. Now, with Gary I couldn't do that.
With Cthulhu it's much easier because if you dare look
upon Him directly, you go insane, which is only fair.

Now for myself, I look at everyone the same, no
matter what. If you need my help you get it. That's
fine for me, as an individual. But I do think that as a
country we have to take care of our own people first.
Driving to work yesterday, I saw three homeless people.
They need our help to get off the street and I know
that my Lord and Master will do that, not just talk
about it like the other candidates. Everywhere He goes
He gathers the lost and the sick and the not-very-fast-
on-their-feet unto Him. He visited our district twice
during the election, and when He was gone there were
literally no people living on the street at all.

I do sometimes read things that He tweets and
yes, I do think, oh my word. I wish I could have just
two minutes with Him to say, 'Master, you need to
straighten up and stop with this foolishness.' But I
don't get offended like some people do. Basically, we
had a choice between the Primal Lurker and Malevo-
lent Entity and a lifelong politician who did her email
wrong. I just couldn't believe her.

You might not like Cthulhu, but even you would

have to concede that when He says He will consume the world, you believe Him.

I feel very, very badly for the people who are scared for their way of life, or even, you know, their actual life. But from what I'm understanding, He's only going to eat illegal immigrants, which everyone agrees with. And I feel bad for the lesbian and gay people and those other ones who can't make up their minds. But from what I also understand, the Elder God is actually in favour of sinful cults so I don't know what they're complaining about.

There's been too much complaining, really. And too much listening to the complaints of other people who aren't me and mine. So, yes. I voted for Cthulhu because I wanted change. I feel the last eight years have been a disgrace. The last president was out for himself. I don't think he really respected the office. I think it was more about him being a celebrity than a president.

Cthulhu doesn't need celebrity. Cthulhu is a Great Old One from the vast deep space between the stars, and I feel like that's what we need to bring our economy back. I don't think left or right or conservative or liberal mean anything to Him, to be quite honest with you. He's not in a box. Mostly He lives in a sunken city of green stone deep beneath the ocean. I don't think He'll take us back to women having no rights or blacks being slaves.

He'll treat everyone the same.

Nobody will have any rights and everyone will be slaves, and that is the fairest way of doing things.

aliensideboob.com, January 2017

The triumph of neo-stupidity

You read this hours before the coronation of an unstable, man-sized shard of penis brittle as the rape-clown-in-chief of the free world. Look around you. The best lack all conviction, while the worst are full of Red Bull and cannibal meth. This surely was a week to ponder what rough beast, its hour come round at last, slouches towards Washington to be born.

Perhaps it'll be just like the final episode of *Buffy* season 3, when the mayor turned into a giant demon snake and tried to eat all the guests. That would be cool, because our very own Senator Malcolm Roberts will be there to represent Pauline Hanson and the 77 lackwits who drooled directly into the ballot box on his behalf. I would totally get up at three in the morning to watch Senator Roberts be eaten by an enormous coil of writhing bowel wearing Donald Trump's face and a burning haystack in place of a hairpiece. Sadly, just because something should happen doesn't mean it will.

I tell my doctor that every time he rings to pester me about my overdue prostate exam.

Roberts and Hanson trolled everyone like champions earlier in the week, fanning themselves with their golden tickets to the crowning of Baron Fuckface von Clownstick as King o' the World. One Nation's Borg Queen twittered like a schoolgirl about being gifted her invite, while Roberts gave the impression he was grinning like your Uncle Bob with a permawoody from mail-order horse viagra.

'Pauline and I received an invitation, but not the Prime Minister,' tweeted the Lesser Malcolm. 'OUCH'.

Cool story, bro.

So much cooler than some desperate fuckdiggler ringing the Aussie embassy again and again begging them to hook him up. Turned out the whole thing was such a fanwank plea-bargain that even the Republican congressman who eventually gave up the tickets felt the need to explainify his role in adding to the number of feral swamp donkeys in the national capital tomorrow.

'Wait. What? Steve Irwin's not coming?'

Why do they do this? Why drop your pants, massage your buttocks with premium cold-pressed olive oil and stand glistening in the bright sun waiting for the giant Dildo of Consequences to ramify the outcomes of your poor choices? And ramify them HARD.

It's a valid question, innit, guv? One the Greater Malcolm might consider as the prime-ministerial

bottom burns red and ever-so-gently quivers in anticipation of the fearful consequences that must come its
way when his debt collectors start going after retirees.

Yes. That's right. Having started the year with a
jumbo-sized bowl of piping hot flop sweat, the bungle-
cunt messiah this week went back for sloppy seconds
on the #notmydebt clusterfuckola, describing his government's aggressive pursuit of billions of dollars it
wasn't owed as 'responsible and appropriate'.

Remember that as you reflect on the poor choices
made by the Lesser Malcolm, who was at least punching up. Or trying to.

The imperial bellends who actually reign over you
did much worse things this week than pathetically big-
ging up their sixth degree of separation from Baron
von Clownstick. They moved to widen the search
for people who didn't owe them any money from the
mentally handicapped and unemployed to the nation's
millions of pensioners. Why? Because those greedy
old fuckers have been living the honky rich life on the
premium tins of dog food and Aldi-brand colostomy
bags while our poor and hungry fucking trough monsters in Canberra have had to travel business class to
each other's wedding and polo orgies.

Business class!

Do you know how embarrassing that is when Lord
Rupert screams past you in his personal jet?

Again, why would anyone who gets elected for a living do this? It can't just be because kicking over some doddering ·wrinklies' walking frames and mugging them for their carefully hoarded stash of dog-food money is easier than going after scary-looking welfare moochers with their Celtic tatts and angry Twitter feeds.

There has to be something deep at work. Something more primal.

And there is. Stupidity.

But not just old-fashioned everyday stupidity. Not just common folly and garden variety derp.

No, this is a sort of amplified neo-stupidity. It's a shameless stupidity that revels in its own asshat-on-backwards majesty. It's networked and self-reinforcing. It's stupidity as an accelerating feedback loop. The kind of stupid that argues for guns in schools to protect against grizzly bear attacks. The kind of stupid that insists, po-faced and pantsless, as Resources Minister Matt Canavan did on Tuesday, that we can reduce our carbon emissions from coal-fired power stations by building more coal-fired power stations. The kind of stupid that took such a fearful fucking beatdown from the last two weeks of #notmydebtpocalypse that it decides hitting itself in the head with a hammer wasn't good enough – it should really frappé its own nads and knob cheese in a giant blender too. Because what could possibly go wrong feeding a couple of million pensioners into the trenches of Centrelink's gigantinormous robot war?

That's the kinda stupidity I'm talkin' about.

And tomorrow it wears a crown.

aliensideboob.com, January 2017

The phone call

Oh man, can you even fucking *imagine* the jet stream of scalding hot piss and vinegar that would've blown Donald Trump's attention-seeking corn-husk wig clean off his skull if Paul Keating had been on that phone call?

You know the one.

The supposed-to-be hour-long scripted reach-around that fell apart as soon as the tangerine Caligula realised some impertinent Crocodile Dundee was trying to stick him with a thousand unwanted darkies and Arabs just one lousy day after he'd signed his bigly popular and even more hugely legal executive order outlawing them.

'This is the worst deal ever,' Trump roared at Turnbull. 'I'm gonna get killed. I had a great solution, a classy solution, and people were gonna love it because Bannon promised me it was a final solution.'

We don't know what Turnbull said, because he's been on heavy trauma medication ever since, but at least we do now understand why he refused to criticise

Trump's Muslim ban. He was terrified that the giant hair plug would renege on the deal Fizza made with the previous president. (Also, it's really hard to speak when your central nervous system's been replaced by a packet of jelly rolls, and at least three of the rolls are missing because George Christensen ate them.)

We'll never know how much of Emperor von Clownstick's angry dick talk was down to being handed a faecal sandwich by Obama, and how much was because Steve Bannon gave him the phone and sneered, 'It's that Aussie asshole whining about some deal again … oh, and he's a *liberal.*'

There is an upside to it, though. The budget deficit be damned; we could pay off the national debt by selling iTunes downloads or CDs of Turnbull's phone call. Stick it up on Spotify. Press some old-school 45 LPs for the collector set. Even more profitable, however, would be coaxing Paul Keating out of his genteel retirement polishing French clocks and listening to Mahler to get on the blower and give Trump an epic serve.

'Shut up. Just sit down and shut up, you pig, you stupid, foul-mouthed grub, you fucking Orobronze dullard. You're not getting out of this deal. You can fucking forget that, you gutless spiv. Get out from under the sunlamp. It's fried your tiny brains so badly you'd be flat out counting past ten. You *are* gonna take these fucking reffos and you'll put 'em up at one of your shitty hotels with full fucking pillow service and a real chocolate mint every night before bedtime if that's what it takes, because if you don't I'm gonna have our submarines drop them all off on the back nine of the golf course at Mar-a-fucking-Lago and don't imagine I'm fucking kidding, mate. You're not tweeting your way out of this one, you slimy fucking zoo penis. From now on, I'm sticking to you like shit to a blanket. By the time I'm finished with you, you'll be nothing but a dead carcass, swinging in the breeze, and nobody will cut you down, and fucking magpies will make a big bloody nest out of that train wreck of a horror mullet you've been trying to pass off as human hair since before the invention of the fucking Hypercolor T-shirt. Got it?'

Or that's what I imagine he might say, anyway. It would probably be much ruder in real life. And Graham Richardson would be there too, gnawing the last shreds of leg meat from Bannon's shattered thigh bones, sucking out the marrow while he waits to eat the Breitbart Nazi's liver with some fava beans and a nice Chianti.

In the world of real things, though, Trump will just bluster and butt-weasel his way out of the agreement. He's all but tweeted his intention of doing so, complaining about Obama taking thousands of 'illegal immigrants' from Australia and threatening to 'study this dumb deal', all of which means Turnbull has to find some other way of avoiding his legal and humanitarian responsibilities. Trump could just say the Iranians, Iraqis and Somalis failed at the 'extreme vetting' stage, but that's not his style. He's more of a fuck-you operator and, having taken Turnbull's unimpressive measure with his own tiny hands, is just as likely to say, well, 'fuck you', and to do it with a misspelled hashtag at three in the morning. Probably during a Twitter feud with Kim Kardashian, the National Park Service and one of those bot accounts that reminds followers to put out the garbage bin.

Lost in the witless hysteria over who hung up on whom is the fate of those thousands of victims of our own xenophobia. (The smart money says Trump got so angry he slammed down the phone and stormed off to get a consolation sandwich, while Turnbull just kept talking and talking until a kindly aide gently pried the phone from his trembling grip and led him away for medication time.) For a little while there it looked as though our imprisoned refugees might catch a break. The chances of that seem vanishingly small now. The deal Obama agreed to is pretty much dead. Even Turnbull has to accept that.

Just as we must accept that Fuckface von Clownstick may be the greatest Russian agent Vladimir

Putin has ever sent into the field. He didn't even need the whole hour to trash the US–Australian alliance. Twenty-five minutes and he was done, and it was sandwich time.

aliensideboob.com, February 2017